RECIPES

FROM THE BARTOLINI

KITCHENS

WITH

MEMORIES OF LIFE IN A TWO-FLAT

ISBN-13: 978-1511849357
ISBN-10: 1511849355

Library of Congress Control Number: 2015913292

CreateSpace Independent Publishing Platform, North Charleston, SC

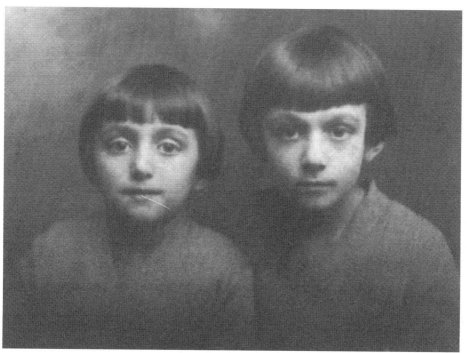

The Bartolini Girls

DEDICATION

This book is dedicated not only to my teachers,
Mom and Zia Lea, the Bartolini Sisters,
but to all 12 who lived under that one roof on Longview Avenue.

TABLE OF CONTENTS

ACKNOWLEDGEMENTS

A book like this cannot be written without the help and support of one's family and friends. This was certainly the case for me. Although I am thankful to all who offered me encouragement and assistance throughout this process, there are a few who deserve special mention.

It is not an exaggeration to state that this book would not have been made without the assistance of my Aunt Lea, *Zia Lea*. She was my primary resource for most of these recipes and many of the stories. Without her, there would be no blog and this book would be little more than a pamphlet. I am very grateful for her love and support.

With special thanks to my fellow residents of the old two-flat. Marina, Paul, Rick, Bill, and Ron all helped me beyond words. Whether they corroborated a story, offered encouragement, or sent photos -- and I did ask again and again (and again!) for more photos -- I knew that I could count on their full support through every step of the process.

Jarod Kintz titled one of his books, *There Are Two Typos Of People In This World: Those Who Can Edit And Those Who Can't* (Kindle, 2010) There should be no doubt that I belong in the latter camp. Luckily, I have two people in my life who are members of the first group and who graciously accepted the challenge of editing my book. Working separately, Donna Carloni and Cecilia M. B. Gunther transformed my draft into the cookbook that lays before you. I will never be able to thank these two miracle workers enough.

INTRODUCTION

Grandpa Bart

OUR ROOTS

Corinaldo

This family cookbook would not be complete without a look at how we Bartolini came to be, eventually living together in that two-flat on Detroit's East Side. We'll start with the patriarch of the Bartolini Clan.

Born in 1898, Amedeo Bartolini, my maternal grandfather - known as *Grandpa* or *Bart* to everyone - came to America from Corinaldo, Italy in the region of Marche when he was 17 years old. As he often explained, he came to America so that he could ride a bicycle. (Apparently, Great-Grandma, *Bisnonna*, wasn't a fan of bike riding.) Originally living in Cincinnati with relatives, Grandpa enlisted and served as a Morse code signalman shortly after the States joined WWI. After the War, he returned briefly to Corinaldo to get married, bringing Grandma Erselia, nee Chiappa, back to live together in Detroit. They had 2 daughters, Lea, my aunt whom I call *Zia*, (1922), and Theresa, my Mom 1924).

Bisnoona

Although Grandpa's family remained in Corinaldo, Grandma's family moved to France in the early 1920s. Grandma and the girls visited them for a couple of years in the latter half of the 1920s. After the Great Depression began, they returned to the States (aboard the Titanic's sister ship, the Olympic) and at some point lived with Grandpa's Uncle Victor. The years passed and eventually the family lived next door to a boarding house.

Nonna and Nonno Amici

My paternal grandparents, Paolo and Armida Amici, nee Ricco, immigrated to this country from San Marino, a republic surrounded by Italy, after WWI. Their first child, my father - Marino - was born in 1920 in Cleveland. Their second child, Adele, was born a year later. In 1922, the family left America to live in France before eventually settling on a farm in San Marino. It was there that Dad's two brothers, Dominic (1933) and Leo (1934), were born. In the 1930s, the fascists were firmly in control of the governments of both Italy and San Marino. Believing that war was inevitable, Nonno (Grandpa Paolo) sent Dad, who was 16 at the time, to live in America, Cleveland specifically. Eventually, Dad moved to Detroit and lived in a boarding house where he met Theresa, one of the Bartolini girls who lived next door. When WWII broke out, Dad enlisted and served as a radioman in the Air Corps, flying missions over what became known as the "Burma Hump." After the War, he returned home, married his girl next door, and they had 3 children together - Paul, John (me), and Marina.

(continued)

Dad's sister and her husband, Nicola, immigrated to NYC, where they raised 3 children, Paolo, Luigi, and Rosa. When Dad's Father passed away in 1960, his Mother immigrated to New York City, living the remainder of her life with Adele and her family.

Coincidentally, Dad's two brothers married on the same day but an ocean apart. Leo married his bride Mariola in Detroit while Dominic married Giuseppina (*Pina*) in San Marino. Both brothers began their marriages in NYC. Leo and Mariola eventually returned to the Motor City to raise their two daughters, Armida and Emanuela. Dominic, however, moved his family, which now included three daughters, Joanne, Marinella, and Diane, back to San Marino where they remain today.

No discussion of my family's roots would be complete without mentioning Zia Lea's husband - Uncle Al - and his family. Also, from Marche, Uncle, his parents - Enrico and Stefanina - and his sister, Lillian, emigrated from Fabriano, Italy to France and then on to Fort Frances, Ontario, Canada. Lilian currently resides in Winnipeg, Manitoba, Canada, where she and husband Albert raised their children, Lorraine, Paul, Victor, and Stefanie. Constantino Fanelli, Stefanina's brother, who everyone called *Zio*, was also a boarder in the house next door to the Bartolini home. Al met Lea during a visit with Zio. Italy's entrance into WWII complicated the young lovers' courtship since crossing the USA/Canada border was restricted. Love conquered all, however, and the couple married in 1944. Together they had three sons, Ron, Bill, and Rick. After I was born, Zia Lea and Uncle All agreed to be my god-parents.

In 1956, my parents, Zia, Uncle Al, and Grandpa Bart bought a two-flat which was once a convent. My five-member family lived on the first floor, while Zia's family of five and Grandpa lived upstairs. Grandma Stefanina - *Nonna* to all six of us kids - came from Canada for visits and lived upstairs, as well. In all, there was often 12 of us living in that two-flat. Little did we know how very lucky we all were.

In the late 1960s, Uncle Al and Zia bought some property about 100 miles north of Detroit in Michigan's "Thumb". In the years following, he designed and built the house to which they would retire in 1975. When my Dad retired in 1985, he and Mom moved to a home along Lake Huron right next door to, who else but, Zia Lea. At 93 years young, Zia still resides there and, with Mom now gone, has been the main resource for most of these recipes and many stories.

The two Bartolini Sisters each had three children. Of those six, three still live within a few miles of the old two-flat. My cousin Bill and I left Michigan within a few months of each other in 1980. He moved to Virginia and I to Chicago. In 2013, my brother Paul and his family set up residence, *The Palazzo Amici*, in Texas. The next generation has spread even further, with addresses stretching from the Southeast to the Pacific Northwest, and a few points in-between.

And to think, all of this was made possible for want of a bicycle ride.

Guaita Tower atop Mt Titano, Republic of San Marino

THE BASICS

Grandma Erselia and Her Girls

TOMATO SAUCE WITH BEEF AND PORK

Back in the old two-flat, each adult was quite capable of making a sauce for pasta. Granted, it was exceptionally rare for one of the men to make a sauce but that doesn't mean each didn't consider himself to be a master chef when it came to making one. Oddly enough, each adult's sauce was as different from the others as the cook who prepared it. In fact, I'd be willing to bet that if it were somehow possible to recreate an individual's sauce, I would still be able to determine who prepared each. Yes, they were that distinctive despite using almost the exact same ingredients. There were minor exceptions - Mom added a dash of nutmeg and Nonna used a bit of marjoram -- but their effect was relatively minor. Even so, it remains a mystery to me how 6 people could have used the same ingredients and achieved such different results.

Today, I add a little wine to my sauce, unlike the others, but the point to all of this is to make clear that there is no one Bartolini sauce. In that spirit, feel free to to add or subtract any ingredient(s) to make this sauce your own.

INGREDIENTS

3 TBS extra virgin olive oil
¾ to 1 lb. ground beef
¾ to 1 lb. ground pork
1 large onion, chopped
6 to 8 cloves garlic, diced
4 TBS fresh parsley, chopped – separated
1 cup dry red wine

10 crimini mushrooms, sliced
4 TBS tomato paste
2 quarts tomatoes or 2 large (28 oz)
     cans, chopped
2 tsp marjoram
4 TBS fresh basil, chopped – separated
salt & pepper

DIRECTIONS

Heat oil in large sauce pan over a med-high heat. Once hot, add beef and pork, season lightly with salt & pepper, and sauté until the liquids run clear and the meat browns.

Add onion, garlic, and half of the parsley. Stir, season lightly with salt & pepper, and continue to sauté until the onion is translucent.

Add the wine and sauté until all but a trace has evaporated.

Optional: Add mushrooms and continue sautéing until soft, about 5 minutes.

Add tomato paste, mix thoroughly, and continue to sauté another 2 minutes.

Add the tomatoes, half the basil, marjoram, and stir to thoroughly combine. Bring to boil and reduce heat to a soft simmer.

Continue to simmer until the sauce deepens in color and thickens — about 2 hours. Stir occasionally.

Remove from heat. Add remaining parsley and basil. Stir to combine.

Sauce is ready for use with your favorite pasta or, once cooled, for storage in your refrigerator or freezer.

MEATLESS TOMATO SAUCE

As good as a tomato sauce with meat can be, sometimes you'll need a sauce that's a bit lighter. Enter the meatless tomato sauce. This one, with its use of red pepper flakes and red wine, is as hearty a sauce as you'll find. Many won't even notice that there is no meat in the pot.

INGREDIENTS

2 TBS extra virgin olive oil
¼ tsp red pepper flakes
3 carrots, chopped
1 celery stalk, chopped
1 medium onion, chopped
  sliced mushrooms -- optional
3 cloves garlic, minced

½ tsp salt
½ tsp pepper
1 TBS fresh parsley, chopped
1 large can (28 oz) crushed tomatoes
1 small can (15 oz) tomato sauce
2 tsp dried marjoram
1 cup dry red wine
1 TBS fresh basil, chopped

DIRECTIONS

Add oil to a medium sauce pan and heat over a med-high heat. Add pepper flakes and cook for 2 minutes.

Place carrots, celery, and onion into a food processor and run until well-chopped. (This will prevent large chunks of carrot, celery, or onion in your sauce.)

Add chopped carrots, onion, and celery to the pan and sauté until the mixture just begins to caramelize, about 8 to 10 minutes. (Optional: add as many sliced mushrooms, as you like, midway through.)

Add garlic, season with salt, pepper, & parsley and sauté for 2 minutes.

Add crushed tomatoes, sauce, marjoram and wine. Stir to thoroughly combine.

Bring to boil, reduce heat to a soft simmer, and cover.

After 45 minutes, remove cover and continue to simmer for another 45 minutes.

Add basil just prior to serving.

MOM'S BROTH - *BRODO*

Living so close to the parish school, we were expected to eat lunch at home for the school was relatively small and there was no cafeteria. So, while our classmates ate at their desks, we raced home where Mom had lunch ready for us. She served us a varied lunch but, as the weather turned colder, soup would play a larger role. It was no coincidence that just as the temperatures began to dip, Mom's old stockpot would make its first appearance. She would warm us all up with bowls of freshly made soup and a *bollito misto* that was made from the boiled meats. Leftover *brodo* was liquid gold in her kitchen, for she not only served it to us for lunch but kept a couple quarts handy for risotto and a host of other recipes. Most importantly, when the services of Dr. Mom were called upon, she often appeared with a mug of brodo in hand and a sympathetic word.

INGREDIENTS

any combination of chicken backs, 2 to 4 chicken thighs, and/or roasted chicken bones.
1 medium-sized beef shank slice or beef "soup bone"
1 large onion, cut into large pieces
2 carrots, coarsely chopped

2 celery stalks with leaves
2 to 4 garlic cloves, smashed
1 tomato, rough chopped
4 to 6 parsley sprigs
4 to 7 quarts of water, depending upon amount of meat used

DIRECTIONS

Add all the ingredients to a large stock pot, and add enough water to cover all the pan's contents by 3 inches, at least. Since this broth may be used in the preparation of other dishes, it's best to postpone adding salt until it's used.

Bring the ingredients to a boil, then reduce heat to a soft simmer. Periodically skim the film off of the surface and discard.

Simmer the broth for 2½ to 3 hours, depending upon how much brodo you're making.

When finished, take off the heat to cool somewhat. Remove the meats and reserve. Pour the broth through a fine mesh strainer, discarding the cooked vegetables and herbs. Depending upon its intended use, you can pour the broth through a clean kitchen towel, resulting in a clearer brodo. Refrigerate.

Refrigeration will cause any fat to gel and float to the surface. Remove it using a slotted spoon. With the fat removed, store the brodo in the refrigerator for a few days, or, in the freezer for several weeks.

Note: Follow this recipe if you have the bones left over from a roast turkey or duck dinner to create a differently flavored stock, as well as a fantastic risotto.

PREPARING VEGETABLES

INGREDIENTS
Approx. 1 lb broccolini -- substitute any vegetable: broccoli, kale, Swiss chard, cauliflower, string beans, asparagus, you get the idea.
olive oil
1 or 2 cloves of garlic, smashed
salt and pepper

DIRECTIONS
Clean and trim the broccolini.

Bring a large pot of salted water to boil.

Add the broccolini and blanch for several minutes. More or less time may will be requited depending upon whether the vegetable is bitter or has unusually thick stalks.

After a few minutes, remove the broccolini and place in an ice bath to stop the cooking process and retain its color.

Place the olive oil in a frypan over med-high heat and, when hot, add the garlic.

Sauté the garlic until brown, though do not burn. Remove and discard the garlic, leaving the oil in the pan.

Add the vegetable to the pan, season with salt and pepper, and sauté until cooked to your liking.

Serve immediately.

While growing up, Mom introduced us to a number of vegetables, with varying degrees of success depending upon the person. For the most part, she used one method when cooking vegetables and it's pretty much the same as is used throughout Italy. I mention this, particularly the latter part, because we Americans tend to like our vegetables to be cooked but with some crispness retained. Well, not to disappoint anyone, but I've eaten my way across Italy a few of times and I've yet to be served a vegetable that was cooked *al dente*. Traditionally speaking, it's just not done, I'm afraid. That doesn't mean, however, that the dishes aren't tasty or are any less desirable. Besides, some, like kale or rapini, may be a little bitter while others, like Swiss chard, may have ribs or stems that are a little tough. This method of cooking will cure some of that.

Although the recipe mentions broccolini specifically, it's the technique and not the vegetable that's important. Briefly, you bring a pot of salted water to boil, blanch the vegetable for a few minutes, and place it in an ice bath before sautéing in garlic-flavored extra virgin olive oil. You may wish to sauté a small onion, depending upon the vegetable. That's it. Easy peasy.

Though the recipe is easy enough, 2 techniques used are priceless. Some object to having garlic pieces in their food. Flavoring the oil with garlic is a great way to get around the problem. Vegetables cooked in a multi-stage process can often lose their coloring and become less appealing. An ice bath is a great way to preserve the green.

BREADING

This is the fabled Bartolini breading and you'll see it used in a number of recipes in this cookbook. With a little practice, you'll learn to vary the oil content depending upon how the dish will be cooked. Breading for grilled fish, for example, should be a little more moist than otherwise. Use lemon juice to do that. Grilled meats, however, may need a little more oil.

INGREDIENTS

1 cup bread crumbs
¼ cup fresh chopped parsley
extra virgin olive oil
salt and pepper to taste

DIRECTIONS

Combine everything but the oil in a bowl and mix well.

Add enough olive oil to fully moisten the mixture without leaving it sopping wet.

MARINADE

This marinade is used whenever meat is grilled or broiled. Pork, beef, veal, and even chicken, taste so much better when allowed to lounge in this marinade for a bit before cooking. For such an easy preparation, it sure does pack a lot of flavor.

INGREDIENTS

1 to 3 cloves garlic, chopped
1 to 2 TBS fresh rosemary, chopped
3 to 4 TBS extra virgin olive oil
1 to 2 TBS fresh lemon juice - optional
salt and pepper to taste

DIRECTIONS

Combine everything but the oil in a bowl and mix well.

Add the oil and stir well.

Pour over meat and allow to marinate for at least 30 minutes before cooking.

PASTA 101

Paul, Marina, and Me (c 1956)

MOM'S PASTA DOUGH

For ages, pasta was made by adding eggs to a hole in the center of a mound of flour and combined to create dough. Rolling pins were then used to roll the dough into thin sheets. Dried for a bit, the sheets were folded repeatedly to make a *sfoglia*, which was then cut using a sharp knife, the noodle's width determining the type of pasta — i.e., thin: *capellini*; wide: *pappardelle*; etc. I well-remember: Mom wielding her rolling pin; dough sheets drying on floured linens covering tabletops, beds, and the backs of chairs; the family dog banished while the dough dried; and, the sound of Mom's knife quickly cutting perfectly sized pasta, while she chatted with whomever entered her kitchen.

This changed in the late 1960s, when our family's first pasta machine was purchased. Soon thereafter, my brother Paul's godmother, Milia, modified the dough recipe to take advantage of a food processor. The mounds and craters of prior generations were replaced by the whirr of Mom's food processor.

None of this sat well with Dad. A bit of a pasta purist, he could tell whether pasta was machine or hand-rolled. As my sister, Marina, recalls, if Dad saw that Mom was going to make pasta that morning, he'd remind her that hand-rolled was best, requesting that she not use her machine. Satisfied, he'd leave for work. His car probably hadn't reached the end of the block before Mom would grab the machine and get to work. At dinner, the hint of a wry smile would grace Mom's face as Dad praised her "hand-rolled pasta."

INGREDIENTS
2¾ to 3 cups all-purpose flour
4 whole large eggs at room temperature + enough water to equal 1 cup of liquid

DIRECTIONS
Place all ingredients in food processor and mix until a ball of dough forms, about 30 seconds. Dough should not stick to your fingers.

Place dough on floured work surface and begin kneading, adding flour or water, in small amounts, as required. Knead until a smooth dough is achieved, at least 5 minutes.

Cover and allow dough to rest for at least 15 minutes. If longer than an hour, place in the refrigerator, removing it 30 minutes before using.

HAND-CUT PASTAS

Throughout much of modern history, the Italian language has had fewer words in its lexicon than most other languages, and that includes its cousins, the Romance Languages. Granted, the gap has lessened over the last century but the fact that it existed at all is because Italian, being an ancient language, was so closely descended from Latin, an even more ancient language of even fewer words. So, when it came to identifying their pasta, Italians didn't usually create new words but named each after the familiar object it resembled, both real and imagined. We Americans know some of their names but that's just the tip of the meatball. There are pastas named after just about anything, from little tongues (*linguine*) to little ears (*orecchiette*). The name can be heavenly, like the hair of an angel (*capelli d'angelo*), or nefarious, like priest chokers (*strozzapreti*). Some look like shoelaces (*stringozzi*), others like twine (*spaghetti*), and still others like ribbons (*fettuccine*). And then there are the shells, be they from the sea (*conchiglie*) or the land (*lumache*). There are the twins (*gemelli*), flowers (*fiori*), little bells (*campanelle*), and little radiators (*radiatori*). And we mustn't overlook *tortellini*, which are said to resemble the navel of Venus. The list goes on and on, far too long to fully explore here but you get my point.

Using the directions I've shared here, you can hand cut any pasta, from angel hair to *pappardelle*. You'll be pleasantly surprised to learn that not only will your pasta be far more tasty than anything you can buy, it will cook in less than half the time.

INGREDIENTS

Mom's pasta dough - p 26

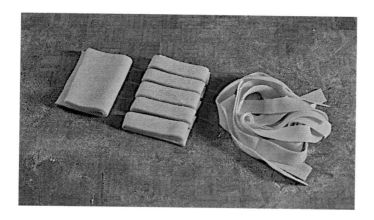

DIRECTIONS

Use a machine or rolling pin to roll the dough till thin, no more than 1/16 inch. On my machine, that's 2 or 3 from its thinnest setting.

Fold the dough in half, from end to end, repeatedly to create a sfoglia that is about 3 to 4 inches wide.

Use a sharp knife to cut the noodles as thin as you like.

Unfurl the pasta and set aside to dry.

AGNOLOTTI

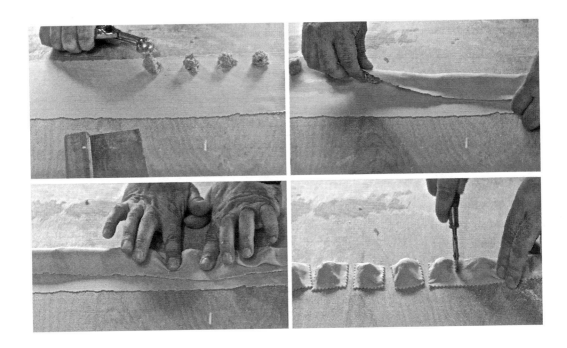

There are a number of stuffed pastas, each with its own point of origin. The region of Piedmont, *Piemonte*, lays claim to *Agnolotti*. The fillings for these pasta pillows are more meat-based than most others and, traditionally, they are often served with a sauce prepared from the drippings resulting from the roasting of those meats. That's not the only way to enjoy them, however, for they are equally delicious when dressed with a burnt butter and sage sauce, or, simply with a bit of your best olive oil and a dusting of grated cheese.

INGREDIENTS

agnolotti filling - p 48
Mom's pasta dough - p 26

DIRECTIONS

Roll a portion of the dough — using a machine or by hand — until quite thin.

Place the dough strip on a lightly floured work surface, Use a pastry cutter to "square off" both ends.

Evenly space balls of filling along one side of the dough strip about a half-inch away from the strip's edge. I use a small ice cream scoop.

Use a pastry brush or your finger tip to lightly moisten the dough on the inner side of the filling,

Carefully fold the dough flap over the filling balls. Make sure the flap touches the filling balls. This will help in the next step.

Use your finger to press the dough between each filling ball before sealing the edge. Try to remove as much of the air as possible.

Use a pastry cutter to cut between each agnolotto and to trim away any excess dough. Place on lightly floured linens or wax paper and use immediately or cover and refrigerate if to be used later that day. I'd recommend freezing them if cooking is to be be delayed much longer.

To cook, bring a large pot of salted water to the boil. Add the agnolotti, lower the heat to a medium simmer, and cook for a few minutes. They will float when cooked but, if in doubt, taste one. It will take a few minutes longer to cook frozen agnolotti.

Gently strain the agnolotti and dress with butter, olive oil, or any number of sauces.

AGNOLOTTI DEL PLIN

INGREDIENTS

agnolotti del plin filling - p 49
Mom's pasta dough - p 26

DIRECTIONS

Take a goose egg-sized piece of dough and roll it until quite thin.

Place the dough strip on a lightly floured work service, trimming both ends to make an elongated rectangle.

Fill a pastry bag with the filling and pipe a line of filling about an inch from the dough strip's edge.

Use a water bottle to mist — or a pastry brush to lightly moisten — the dough on the side of the filling farthest from you. Do not get it too wet or it may split during subsequent steps.

Carefully take hold of the dough's edge and pull it over the piped filling.

Use your fingers to press/seal the flap to the moistened dough, eliminating as much air as possible as you work you way down the strip.

Use your index fingers and thumbs to pinch the filling roll at one inch intervals.

Use a pastry wheel or very sharp knife to first trim away the excess dough

Use the same tool to cut the agnolotti at the center of each pinch.

Place the agnolotti in a single layer on a baking sheet that has been dusted with corn meal or flour. Cover with a clean kitchen towel. If they are to be cooked relatively quickly, nothing further needs to be done. If they are to be cooked in a couple of hours, they should be placed in the fridge until dinner time. If they are to be cooked later than that evening, place the baking sheet in the freezer and, once frozen, place the agnolotti in bags or some other container suitable for freezing.

All agnolotti originated in Piedmont. They are that region's ravioli. Agnolotti del Plin are so named because the individual pasta pillows are pinched, *plin*, when made. Because of this, the filling needs to be softer than most and a pastry bag can be used to create them, as you can see below.

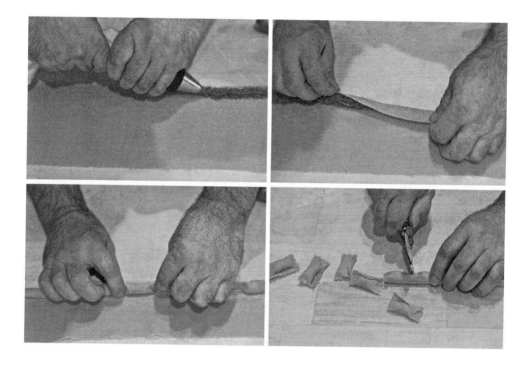

FAZZOLETTI

Fazzoletti, "little handkerchiefs", are among the easiest of pastas to make at home. In fact, it will take you far longer to make the pasta dough and roll it out than it will for you to make these little squares.

INGREDIENTS

Mom's pasta dough - p 26

DIRECTIONS

Using a rolling pin or pasta machine, roll the dough until thin. I usually go to the No 6 or 7 setting on my rollers, where 1 is the widest setting.

Use a straight edge/ruler to cut equally sized squares from the dough strips. You can cut them as large as you like, though I prefer mine to be about 2 inches square.

Place the fazzoletti on a floured linen or wax paper, cover with a clean cloth, for use later that afternoon.

To cook, place in rapidly boiling salted water. Cook until al dente, about 3 minutes. Taste if uncertain.

Drain the pasta and dress with the sauce of your preference.

MALTAGLIATI

Maltagliati is a pasta of irregular shapes, the name of which is derived from the Italian words for badly cut, *male taglio*. It is the end pieces and leftover bits of pasta that result from a day of pasta making. Like snowflakes, no two pieces are alike, each being randomly cut. The fact that there would be enough scraps to prepare a dinner is an indication of the difference between our two countries' eating habits. Rarely would any of us today have enough scraps to create a single serving of pasta, let alone enough for a family. That's OK. We'll fake it and create a pasta that looks like random bits and pieces.

INGREDIENTS

Mom's pasta dough - p 26

DIRECTIONS

Roll out a bit of pastry dough, by hand or machine, as thin as you like.

Using a pastry cutter, cut strip of pasta dough into pieces, varying them as much as you like. Remember, they are to look "badly formed". Perfection is not the goal.

Lay to dry on a lightly floured linens or sheet pans lined with wax paper.

Cook as you would any pasta, in heavily salted boiling water.

GARGANELLI

Similar in shape to *penne*, garganelli are a tubular pasta that come from the Emilia-Romagna region of Italy. With Bologna as its capital, Emilia-Romagna is known for its hearty meat sauces. (*Ragu alla Bolognese*, anyone?) Garganelli, like penne, is particularly well-suited for such sauces and its use has spread to other areas of Italy because of that. Garganelli was also immortalized in the movie *Big Night* (1996), in which it was handmade in preparation for the film's climactic feast.

Whereas it's quite difficult to create perfect penne by hand, garganelli is very often handmade and has a "flap" where the pasta is joined to create the tube. Just like *penne rigate*, garganelli traditionally have ridges on each tube's outer surface; the better to hold on to that rich tomato sauce. Now, you can search the web and you'll find little boards made just for putting ridges on your garganelli, but not me. Years ago, much to the amusement of Mom & Zia, I bought a gnocchi board that is used to put ridges on gnocchi. (In my defense, I needed a few more dollars in my order to qualify for free shipping and a gnocchi board was just the ticket.) As you'll soon see and as I was quick to point out to Zia, putting ridges on garganelli is yet another (of two) uses for this wonderful kitchen gadget. Now, don't fret if you haven't this nifty little gizmo taking up space in a junk drawer. You can just as easily use the back of a fork, like you would when making gnocchi, or leave them smooth, like normal penne. No matter. Don't let the absence of a few ridges cause you to miss out on this great tasting pasta.

INGREDIENTS

Mom's pasta dough - p 26

DIRECTIONS

Roll the dough to a thickness of 6 or 7 on a pasta machine, where 1 is the widest setting.

Use a straight edge and pastry cutter to cut the strip into 2 inch squares.

Place each square on a gnocchi board or work surface and lightly moisten the top OR lower corner.

Using a dowel or thin rod, roll the dough sheet toward the moistened corner, gently pressing the pasta sheet. If using a gnocchi board, this will create ridges on the newly forming tube. Otherwise, roll the tube over the back of a fork to create the ridges. Of course, you don't have to make ridges at all, if that's your preference.

Set aside to dry or use with your favorite sauce.

ORECCHIETTE

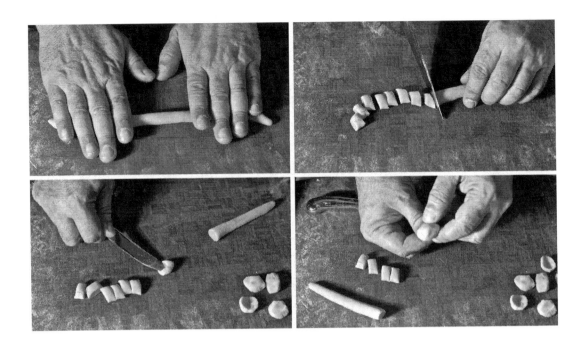

This pasta comes to us from Puglia, *Apulia*, a region along Italy's Southeast coast, including the "heel of the boot". Meaning little ears, orecchiette is another pasta named for that which it resembles. And if you're willing to accept that *tortellini* were modeled after the navel of Venus, you should have no problem accepting that orecchiette look like little ears.

Coming from Southern Italy, it's a safe bet to say that the dough should be made with durum flour and water. And if you want to make authentic orecchiette, that's what you should do. The fact is that we Bartolini came from the Marche region where eggs are used to make pasta. That's how I learned to make pasta dough and that's the recipe I shared earlier. Now, I've tried to make pasta using durum floirc but certainly not enough times to get a "feel" for the dough like I have with Mom's pasta dough. So, though this pasta shape is *Pugliese*, from Puglia, the pasta dough is *Marchigiani*, from Marche.

INGREDIENTS

Mom's pasta dough - p 26

DIRECTIONS

Take a piece of dough and roll it into a ball about the size of a golf ball. Be sure to cover the remaining dough to prevent it from drying out.

Roll out a "snake" about ⅓ to ½ inch wide.

Cut the dough into equally sized segments of about ½ inch in length.

Using the tip of a blunt knife, smash the dough segment and draw it towards you. This will flatten the segment and cause it to curl over the knife. Keep a supply of flour nearby to occasionally coat the tip of the knife.

Invert the curled segment, pulling it over your thumb in the process.

Once removed from your thumb tip, you'll have a perfectly shaped orecchietta.

Cook in boiling salted water as you would any pasta.

QUADRETTI PASTA

Generally speaking, when I wasn't feeling well, Mom relied upon 3 dishes to get me up-and-about. Breakfast would be a 3-minute egg, with or without buttered toast depending upon my stomach's attitude. My meals would be *pasta in bianco,* pasta simple dressed with butter and a sprinkling of cheese. Aside from it being a traditional cure served to *bambini* with stomach ailments, Mom knew that I could have been at Death's Door and I would have agreed to at least try a little pasta in bianco. Between meals, though, there was a constant supply of broth which, as the recovery progressed, contained more and more *pastine*. This is where Mom's therapy varied, based upon the child. Ask Sis what Mom served her when ill and she'll mention, without hesitation, *Acini di Pepe*, a tiny bead-like pasta. As for my Brother Paul and me, it was *quadretti* all the way.

Quadretti are a square-shaped pastina that are quite easy to make. Whenever Mom made pasta of any kind, she would roll out the leftover dough and use it to make quadretti. (In true Italian tradition, absolutely nothing was wasted.) This she stored in a container, adding to it with each new batch of homemade pasta. Because she was always adding to her stash, she rarely had to devote a batch of pasta dough to making quadretti. When combined with the quart or 2 of chicken stock she was sure to have on-hand for risotto, Mom was always prepared when one of us was feeling under the weather.

INGREDIENTS

Mom's broth - p 19
Mom's pasta dough - p 26

DIRECTIONS

Take a sheet of thinly rolled pasta.

Fold it repeatedly in half, end to end, until it is about 4 inches wide. This is called a sfoglia.

Use a sharp knife to cut the folded dough into strips about the width of linguine.

Carefully turn a number of the strips 90 degrees.

Cut the strips about the same width, creating tiny squares.

Set aside to dry completely before storing in a covered container.

To Serve: bring a pot of stock to boil, add the quadretti pasta, and simmer until cooked to your liking.

RAVIOLI

INGREDIENTS

Mom's pasta dough - p 26
ravioli filling - pp 51, 52, 53, 55, 56, also 48 & 50

DIRECTIONS

Roll a goose egg-sized piece of dough until within 2 or 3 of the rollers thinnest setting.

Flour the ravioli mold and trim two dough sheets so that both are of equal length and extend about an inch on either end of the mold.

Cover the mold with one dough sheet. Press down lightly on the indentations in the sheet.

Place a small amount of filling in each indentation, being careful not to use too much.

Use a pastry brush dampened with water to lightly moisten the edges of each raviolo.

Use the second dough sheet to completely cover the mould and fillings.

Use a rolling pin to go over the mold, pressing firmly to seal the pasta pillows.

Trim off the excess dough and flip the mold to release the ravioli.

Place in a single layer on lightly floured table linens or wax paper before covering with a cloth.

Either cook within hours or refrigerate/freeze for use beyond that day.

It wasn't Christmas or any holiday without a platter of ravioli serving as centerpiece. In my eyes, nothing else mattered and I hoped everyone seated at the table ate the other, "filler," dishes that Mom had prepared, leaving more ravioli for me. Once I moved away from home, it was my love of Mom's ravioli that started me on the path to cooking our family recipes. Three hundred miles was just too far to drive for a ravioli dinner.

The instructions detailed here can be used to make *cappelletti,* as well. The only differences between the two being their fillings and size. Being a soup ravioli, cappelletti are smaller and one *cappelletto* should easily fit on a soup spoon. I use my smallest mold to make them.

STROZZAPRETI

Zia and I were in Florence in 2002 and shared a laugh when a waiter told us a legend behind this pasta's name. At the time, however, I mistakenly thought that he was merely giving us a sales pitch. According to the waiter, strozzapreti is so good that when it was invented and first served to priests, they devoured it so quickly that they choked. You must admit, if you're trying to sell pasta, that's a pretty good story to have up your sleeve. Move forward a few years. I'd forgotten all about the pasta until I heard some chef on television mention priests choking. After some web searching, I saw how the pasta was made and strozzapreti became a part of my pasta arsenal.

Strozzapreti are a twisted pasta, about 3 inches in length, vaguely reminiscent of *cavatelli*. Of course, cavatelli, being machine-made, are consistent in shape and length, while homemade strozzapreti are anything but — and therein lies its charm. Few would ever mistake a dish of homemade strozzapreti for a mass-produced pasta and no mass-produced pasta will ever taste nearly as good as homemade strozzapreti. The latter part of that statement is as good a reason as any for taking the time to make this pasta.

INGREDIENTS

Mom's pasta dough - p 26

DIRECTIONS

Create a sfoglia by taking a 12 inch strip of thin pasta dough and folding it in half, end to end repeatedly, until it is about 3 inches wide.

Use a sharp knife to cut the strip into pasta as wide as tagliatelle - about ⅓ inch wide.

Unfurl one noodle and place its tip at the base of your palm.

Rub you hands together causing the noodle to twist in the process.

Cut the now twisted pasta into pieces about 3 inches in length.

Cook as you would any fresh pasta, dressing it with the sauce of your choice once you've drained the pasta fully.

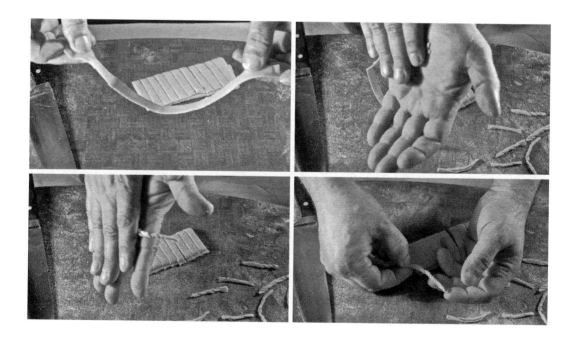

GNOCCHI

Gnocchi were among the first things we kids were allowed to help Mom prepare in the kitchen. She and Zia would make the dough and then hand us kids a piece to roll into a log, though we called them snakes. With a butter knife we were taught how to cut the snake and, depending upon our age, we might even have been allowed to try to roll them across a fork's tines to make the grooves. Granted, our gnocchi weren't perfect but that really didn't matter. After all, if your homemade pasta looks too perfect, no one will ever believe that they were made by hand. Believe me, no one ever thought our gnocchi were store bought.

INGREDIENTS

2 large russet potatoes, once cooked,
    peeled, & riced - approx. 18 oz
a little more than a cup all-purpose flour
1 large egg, slightly beaten
corn meal or additional flour for dusting
    surfaces

DIRECTIONS

Pre-heat oven to 400° F. Use a fork to pierce the potatoes numerous times.

Place the potatoes on center rack and bake until cooked, from 50 to 60 minutes, depending upon the potato size.

Meanwhile, gather the other ingredients. Allow the egg to come to room temperature.

Once cooked, remove potatoes and set aside until they can be safely handled.

Slice each potato in half lengthwise and use a spoon to scoop out all of the potato, reserving the skins for some other purpose.

Run the cooked potatoes through a ricer or food mill.

Use the riced potatoes to create a mound on a floured work surface.. Make a well in the center of the mound, as you would when making pasta dough.

Sprinkle the top of the well's walls with ¾ cup flour. Place the egg in the center well after the potato has cooled enough so that the egg won't cook.

Using a fork, slowly combine the potato and flour with the egg. Once the dough renders the fork useless, continue mixing with your hands.

Dough should come together within 4 to 5 minutes. It will be ready when it is firm and a little moist to the touch without being tacky. Add more flour as needed but keep in mind that the less flour used, the better.

Form a ball with the dough and divide it into fourths.

Take a quarter and divide it in half. Roll one of the sections into a log with a width of you preference. We normally roll them about an inch wide -- the width of an index finger.

Use a sharp knife or board scraper to cut the log into segments, each ½ to an inch long.

If grooves are desired: flour the back of a dinner fork, place a segment at the top of the tines, use your finger to roll it over the tines, creating gnocchi with grooves on one side and a dimple where your finger rolled it.

If grooves aren't wanted: use a finger to push and roll each segment across the work surface, creating smooth surfaced gnocchi with dimples where you'd placed your fingers.

Place the gnocchi on a lined baking sheet that's been dusted with flour or corn meal.

If not going to be cooked within a few hours, place the gnocchi-covered baking sheet in a freezer and once the gnocchi are frozen solid, place them in containers/bags suitable for freezer storage.

NOTES

Making gnocchi is not an exact science. I bake the potatoes so that they will be drier and require less flour. Remember, the less flour used, the better your gnocchi will be. If your gnocchi are too heavy and dense, chances are you've used too much flour.

Mom always used her tomato sauce with meat to dress gnocchi. You, too, can do that, or, you can go to **Sauces** and give the **Gorgonzola Sauce** recipe - p 69 - a try. It's a great way to enjoy these little dumplings.

STUFFED PASTA FILLINGS

Cousins Ron, Rick, and Bill (c 1960)

AGNOLOTTI FILLING

While in Bologna, I dined at a restaurant that was a favorite among the locals. I ordered tortellini served in a cream sauce and asked my waiter about the filling. His English was limited and he left to retrieve the Sous Chef. This very generous Sous Chef gave me the recipe, explaining that it was used in the tortellini but it was really a traditional agnolotti filling - her family's.

INGREDIENTS

2 tbs butter
8 oz veal
8 oz prosciutto crudo
8 oz prosciutto cotto
8 oz mortadella

4 oz grated Parmigiano Reggiano
nutmeg, salt and pepper, to taste
1 egg, slightly beaten

DIRECTIONS

In a frypan over med-high heat, melt the butter before adding the veal pieces. Season lightly with salt and pepper and sauté until browned on all sides. Set aside.

Cut both types of prosciutto and the mortadella into cubes. Grind the 4 meats using the meat grinder plate with the smallest holes.

Once all have been ground, add the grated cheese and nutmeg, mix well, and taste to check seasoning. Add nutmeg, salt and pepper, if needed.

Add the egg and mix until combined.

Cover and refrigerate for several hours or overnight before using.

See page 28 to learn how to make Agnolotti.

Notes:
This filling can, also, be used to make ravioli - p 40

Traditionally, the veal is roasted before being ground. Since I was preparing a relatively small number of agnolotti, I sautéed the veal instead.

AGNOLOTTI DEL PLIN FILLING

I created this filling so that I could experiment with the technique for making Agnolotti del Plin. The tests were a big success. The filling is delicious and one that I continue to make.

INGREDIENTS

1½ TBS butter
1½ TBS olive oil
1 large (1.5 oz,) shallot, diced
3.5 oz Tuscan kale (cavolo nero),
    trimmed of thick ribs — any kale
    may be substituted,
2 TBS butter

1 lb chicken gizzards trimmed and
    chopped
1 cup ricotta cheese
½ cup grated Pecorino Romano cheese
nutmeg
1 large egg
salt and pepper

DIRECTIONS

Heat equal parts butter and olive oil (no more than 3 TBS total) in a deep frying pan over med-high heat. Once hot, add the shallot and sauté until translucent – about 3 minutes.

Meanwhile, roughly chop the cleaned & trimmed kale leaves before placing them in the pan with the shallots. Season lightly with salt & pepper and sauté until wilted.

Allow to cool and drain as much liquid as possible from the cooked kale before placing it in a clean kitchen towel. Wring out as much liquid as possible. Set aside.

In the same frying pan, melt another 2 TBS butter over medium heat. Add the chicken gizzards, season with salt and pepper, and sauté until fully cooked – about 20 to 25 minutes. Remove from heat and allow to cool.

Once cooled, place the cooked gizzards into a food processor and process until well ground.

To the chopped gizzards in the food processor, add the cooked kale, ricotta cheese, Pecorino Romano cheese, egg, nutmeg to taste, and season lightly with salt & pepper. Process until smooth.

Remove and refrigerate several hours or overnight so that the flavors will blend.

See page 30 to learn how to make Agnolotti del Plin.

Note: This filling can, also, be used to make ravioli - p 40.

SAUSAGE RAVIOLI FILLING

Who doesn't like a serving of good sausage ravioli? Though admittedly biased, you won't find better than these made with our family's sausage. Of course, you can substitute any sausage but why would you want to?

INGREDIENTS

1 lb Bartolini sausage meat - p 154
1 pkg (10 oz) frozen chopped spinach, cooked and well-drained
1 cup ricotta
1 cup grated Pecorino Romano cheese
1 egg, slightly beaten

DIRECTIONS

Sauté meat over med-high heat until browned.

Use meat grinder to finely process the meat. Drain any excess juices.

Add all the ingredients into a mixing bowl and mix until well-combined.

Cover and refrigerate for several hours or overnight before using.

See page 40 to learn how to make Ravioli.

PORK AND VEAL RAVIOLI FILLING

This is the recipe for the filling for traditional Bartolini ravioli and, coincidentally, a favorite snack for my dog, Max. Once, after an afternoon spent making ravioli -- we called it Ravioli Day -- we noticed that we were short several ravioli. When we make ravioli, Zia and I use molds that produce 12 ravioli at a time. So long as we fill every mold used, we should end up with a multiple of 12 when we count them. Well, we didn't. In fact, we were short 6 ravioli. That evening, while my cousin Ron, AKA the Max Whisperer, and I enjoyed our afternoon Manhattan, I glanced at the pasta board in the next room. There was Max closing in on the ravioli that were meant for our dinner. In the time it took me to shout, "Max!", he had vacuumed 35 of the pasta pillows. 35! Not only was the mystery of the vanishing ravioli solved but, I'm happy to report, those are the last ravioli he's stolen -- but it's not for a lack of trying.

INGREDIENTS

2 to 3 TBS butter
1½ lbs. pork
1½ lbs. veal (chicken may be
    substituted)
1 pkg (10 oz) chopped spinach - cooked
    and well-drained

1 pkg (8 oz) cream cheese
1 cup grated Pecorino Romano or
    Parmigiano Reggiano cheese –
    your choice
2 or 3 eggs slightly beaten
dash of cloves (optional)

DIRECTIONS

Melt butter in a frypan over medium heat.

Add the meat, sauté until brown, and season lightly with salt.

Use a meat grinder or food processor to mince the meats. Drain any excess juices.

Add all the ingredients into a mixing bowl and mix until well-combined.

Cover and refrigerate for several hours or overnight before using.

See page 40 to learn how to make Ravioli.

RICOTTA, ASPARAGUS, AND CRIMINI MUSHROOM RAVIOLI FILLING

This is a ravioli *primavera* and takes advantage of spring's first offerings. Talk about a treat!

INGREDIENTS

1 TBS olive oil
1 TBS butter
8 oz fresh asparagus
8 oz fresh crimini mushrooms
3 oz spring onions
2 garlic cloves, minced or grated
½ tsp kosher salt
⅛ tsp white pepper
zest of ½ lemon
¾ cup (12 oz) ricotta, well-drained
½ cup grated Pecorino Roman cheese,
Parmigiano may be substituted

DIRECTIONS

Clean and roughly chop the asparagus, mushrooms, onion, & garlic

Heat olive oil and butter over med-high heat. Add asparagus, mushroom, and onion, lower heat to medium, and sauté until mixture just begins to change color — about 6 or 7 minutes.

Add garlic, salt, and pepper, and continue to sauté until liquids are gone. Do not allow to burn.

Remove from heat and allow to cool fully before proceeding.

If using a food processor: Place the asparagus mixture into the processor, add the lemon zest, ricotta and Romano cheeses, and process until uniformly smooth.

If not using a food processor: Chop the asparagus mixture as finely as possible. Add the zest and cheeses and stir to thoroughly combine.

Cover the filling and refrigerate for a few hours or overnight.

See page 40 to learn how to make Ravioli.

CANNELLONI AND CAPPELLETTI FILLING

Yes, the same filling is used for both pastas. You may wish to try using the Bartolini ravioli filling recipe - p 52 - for cannelloni, too.

INGREDIENTS

2 to 3 TBS butter
1½ lbs. pork
1½ lbs. veal (chicken may be
    substituted)
1 pkg (8 oz) cream cheese

1 cup grated Pecorino Romano —
    Parmigiano may be used
2 or 3 eggs slightly beaten — depending
    on size
¼ tsp ground nutmeg
zest of 1 lemon, more if you like

DIRECTIONS

Melt butter in a sauté pan over med-high heat.

Add meat and sauté until browned. Season lightly with salt.

Use a meat grinder or food processor to mince the meats. Drain any excess juices.

Add all the ingredients into a mixing bowl and mix until well-combined.

Cover and refrigerate for several hours or overnight before using.

See page 40 to learn how to make Cappelletti and page 102 to learn how to make Cannelloni.

GOAT CHEESE, LEEK, AND PORCINI MUSHROOM RAVIOLI FILLING

This ravioli's main ingredients were all purchased at the farmer's market that morning. Now that's fresh!

INGREDIENTS

.7 oz dried porcini mushrooms
1 TBS olive oil
1 TBS butter
3 oz leeks, chopped fine
1 garlic clove, minced or grated
½ tsp kosher salt
⅛ tsp white pepper
10.5 oz goat cheese

DIRECTIONS

Allow mushrooms to soak in very hot water for at least 20 minutes.

Remove mushrooms to paper towels, being careful not to disturb sediments in the liquid. Use another paper towel to blot the mushrooms dry before chopping them to a small dice. Put aside.

Heat olive oil and butter over med-high heat. Add leeks and mushrooms, lower heat to medium, and sauté until mixture just begins to change color — about 6 or 7 minutes.

Add garlic, salt, and pepper, and continue to sauté until liquids are gone. Do not allow to burn.

Remove from heat and allow to cool fully before proceeding.

Once cooled, combine mushroom-leek mixture and goat cheese and stir to thoroughly combine.

Cover and refrigerate for several hours or overnight before using.

See page 40 to learn how to make Ravioli

Note: Liquid used to hydrate mushrooms can be strained and saved for use when making soups or risotto

ROAST DUCK RAVIOLI FILLING

Zia and I created this filling recipe using the leftovers from a duck we roasted together (p 164). It makes a very tasty ravioli and is reminiscent of the origins of many of Italy's stuffed pastas. It wasn't so very long ago where meat was rarely served outside of holidays or festive occasions. Seldom was there enough meat left over for another meal and, without refrigeration, it needed to be used as soon as possible. By combining the meat with several other ingredients and using it as filling, that little bit of meat could be stretched to feed the family another time.

By the way, the bones from that duck were used to make stock which, in turn, was used to make risotto. That recipe can be found on p 116.

INGREDIENTS

2 large red onions, sliced
2 TBS butter
extra virgin olive oil
Marsala wine
10 oz rapini (broccoli raab)

9 oz skinless roast duck, shredded
1 cup ricotta, drained
½ cup Pecorino Romano cheese, grated
1 large egg
salt & pepper, to taste

DIRECTIONS

Melt butter in a large fry pan over medium heat. Add onions and stir to coat with the butter.

Sauté for about 10 minutes, season lightly with salt and pepper, lower to med-low heat, and continue to cook, stirring frequently. You want the onions to brown but not burn. Be patient. The onions will take at least an additional 20 minutes to caramelize. Add a little bit of olive oil if the onions are too dry.

Just before the onions are ready, deglaze the pan with a couple ounces of Marsala wine. The onions will be ready when the wine has evaporated.

Once the onions have cooled, drain any excess oils before placing them in a clean kitchen towel, wringing out as much moisture as possible.

Meanwhile, bring a large pot of lightly salted water to the boil.

Add the rapini and, once the boil returns, blanch the rapini for 5 minutes.

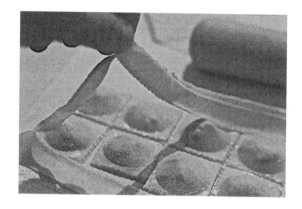

Remove the rapini from the boiling water and immediately plunge the vegetable into an ice water bath.

Once fully cooled, drain the rapini of as much liquid as possible before wringing in a clean kitchen towel.

Use a meat grinder — or food processor — to grind the duck, caramelized onions, and blanched rapini.

Add the Pecorino Romano and ricotta cheeses to the mince and stir well.

Taste to check for seasoning before adding the egg. Stir until well-combined, cover, and refrigerate for a few hours or overnight before using.

See page 40 to learn how to make Ravioli.

SAUCES

Zia Lea
Mom   *At school in France*

CREAM SAUCES

As much as I may enjoy a good tomato-based sauce for my pasta, some dishes are better served with a cream sauce. Quick and easy to prepare, rather than list them all individually, I thought it best to group them here, under one heading. After all, they are quite similar, as you'll soon see. The recipes will use as few as 2, or as many as all, of the listed ingredients. No amounts are listed because they will depend upon the amount of pasta being prepared. Of course, salt and pepper should be added, to taste.

There is a fourth cream sauce, one that uses vodka. Utilizing more ingredients, it's not quite as easy to prepare as these 3 and, for that reason, has been separated from the rest. You can find the recipe at the end of this chapter on p 70.

INGREDIENTS

heavy cream - if milk or half-and-half is used, it will take longer to reduce
butter, the amount of which will depend upon the recipe
grated cheese -- Pecorino Romano or Parmigiano Reggiano, your preference
tomato sauce or tomato paste

nutmeg though not listed below, can be added to any of the sauces, depending upon the pasta being served. Remember that a little bit goes a very long way.

DIRECTIONS

A) PLAIN CREAM SAUCE

As the name suggests, place heavy cream in a sauce pan and reduce until half in volume. Use to dress the pasta, garnished with grated cheese.

B) CREAM, BUTTER, AND CHEESE SAUCE

Place heavy cream in a sauce pan and reduce until half in volume. Add butter and grated cheese to the pan. Together, they should equal half the volume of the now-reduced cream. Use to dress the pasta, garnished with grated cheese.

C) PINK SAUCE

Prepare the cream sauce (B above) and add ¼ cup of plain tomato sauce or 2 TBS tomato paste. The end result should be pink, not red, and the tomato should enhance, not bury, the sauce's flavors.

PESTO GENOVESE

Pesto was one of those dishes that I had enjoyed eating but never thought to make myself. Several years ago, before I moved to my present home, a good friend taught me how to make pesto using basil grown in my garden. I haven't bought another drop since. Sure, we all know that pesto is great when combined with hot pasta but that's only part of the story. Pesto-dressed pasta can also be served at room temperature and, if chilled, the addition of a few ingredients will make a great pasta salad. Moving beyond pasta, I'll use a couple of tablespoons of pesto to flavor soups, sauces, in sandwiches, and in meat marinades. When roasting a chicken or game hen, a little pesto between the bird's flesh and skin results in a very flavorful main course. The fact is that pesto isn't just for pasta anymore.

As easy as pesto is to prepare, there are a few things to remember. First off, be sure to use only fresh ingredients. This is not the time to use dried basil or powdered garlic. Traditionally, pesto is made with a mortar and pestle and some swear by it. I use a food processor to make my pesto but a high-speed blender may be used, as well. No matter how you prepare it, do not over-process the basil. If you do, your basil will darken considerably. Lastly, pesto can be stored in the fridge for up to one week and frozen for much longer. When I freeze pesto, I do not add any cheese to the processor. I find that pesto thaws better when there is no cheese in the mix. When I go to use the pesto, I mix it into the pasta and add as much cheese as needed. Additionally, when I freeze pesto, I'll do so in ice cube trays and then place the frozen cubes in bags for storage. Doing so will ensure that you'll defrost only what you need.

INGREDIENTS

¼ cup pine nuts

2 to 3 cloves garlic, roughly chopped

2 cups basil leaves, about 2 oz by weight

¼ tsp salt

pepper to taste

½ to ¾ cup extra virgin olive oil

⅓ cup parmesan cheese

DIRECTIONS

Add the pine nuts and garlic to your food processor or blender.

Process about 20 seconds to chop the ingredients.

Add the basil, salt, and pepper and pulse for a few seconds, about 3 or 4 times. This should give the basil a rough chop.

Start the processor and pour the olive oil through the feed tube in a slow, steady stream. Stop the processor about 5 seconds after all the oil has been added.

At this point, the pesto may be frozen for later use.

If you are not going to freeze the pesto, add the grated cheese and process just long enough to combine the ingredients.

Pesto is now ready and may be used to dress your favorite pasta, etc.

RAGU ALLA BOLOGNESE

Many consider a Bolognese sauce as a tomato sauce that has some meat when, in fact, it's quite the opposite. A true Bolognese is meat with a bit of tomato. To that end, I've included beef, veal, pork, sausage, and pancetta in my recipe and only tomato paste will be used. Most Bolognese feature relatively few spices and herbs, although I've included a couple because that's just the way we Bartolini roll. Unique to a Bolognese, some form of dairy is added to the pot, though the timing may vary. I use a good amount early in the preparation. Lastly, wine is added early on and though I choose to use a dry white, you may wish to use a red instead.

INGREDIENTS

1 large onion
2 to 3 carrots
2 to 3 celery stalks
6 cloves garlic, diced
4 TBS fresh parsley, chopped
3 TBS extra virgin olive oil
¾ to 1 lb. ground beef
¾ to 1 lb. ground pork
¾ to 1 lb. ground veal
4 oz ground pancetta

6 oz pork sausage - p 154
1 cup dry white wine
12 oz half-and-half (whole milk or a mixture of whole milk & heavy cream may be substituted)
1 can (12 oz,) tomato paste
2 cups low sodium beef stock
salt & pepper

DIRECTIONS

Use a food processor to finely chop the carrots, onion, celery, garlic, and parsley.

Meanwhile, heat the oil in a sauce pan over med-high heat.

Add the chopped vegetable mixture to the hot oil, season lightly with salt and pepper, and sauté until the vegetables start to color.

Add the ground meats, stir well, and continue to sauté until the juices run clear and the meat has darkened due to caramelization.

Add the milk and cook until half has evaporated. Add tomato paste, mix thoroughly, and continue to sauté another 2 minutes then add the wine and sauté until most has evaporated - usually no more than 5 minutes.

Add the beef stock, stir well, bring to a boil, and reduce to a low simmer.

Continue to simmer until the sauce deepens in color and thickens — at least 2½ to 3 hours. Stir occasionally. At the end, season with salt and pepper, to taste. Sauce is ready for use with your favorite pasta or, once cooled, for storage in your refrigerator or freezer.

TOMATO SAUCE WITH BOAR

During a recent trip to Italy, all three of us, my good friends Gail, David, and I, noticed that virtually every restaurant we entered had boar meat of some sort on the menu. I don't recall ever seeing it so widely used in prior trips. Upon returning home, I was very happy to see that a local grocery store was now offering ground boar meat. Granted, I would prefer to grind it myself but we'll take things one step at a time.

To prepare this sauce, I used elements of both, our basic meat sauce (p 16) and the Bolognese (p 64), the object being to create a sauce that preserves the rich flavor of boar as much as possible.

INGREDIENTS

1 medium onion
1 carrot
1 celery stalk
2 cloves garlic
2 TBS fresh parsley
3 TBS extra virgin olive oil

1 lb ground boar
4 oz half-and-half
2 TBS tomato paste
1 cup dry white wine
1 can (14 oz) diced tomatoes
1 cup water
salt & pepper

DIRECTIONS

Use a food processor to finely chop the onions, carrots, celery, garlic, and parsley.

Meanwhile, heat the oil in a sauce pan over med-high heat.

Add the chopped vegetable mixture to the hot oil, season with lightly with salt and pepper, and sauté until the vegetables begin to color.

Add the ground boar, stir well, and continue to sauté until the juices run clear and the meat has darkened due to caramelization.

Add the half-and-half and cook until half has evaporated. Add tomato paste, mix thoroughly, and continue to sauté another 2 minutes before adding the wine. Continue to sauté until most has evaporated.

Add the tomatoes and water, stir well, bring to a boil, and reduce to a low simmer.

Continue to simmer until the sauce deepens in color and thickens — about 60 to 90 minutes. Stir occasionally.

Taste to see if salt and pepper are needed.

Sauce is ready for use with your favorite pasta or, once cooled, for storage in your refrigerator or freezer.

TOMATO SAUCE WITH TUNA

This simple tomato sauce relies upon tuna as its protein and, being Catholic, was a staple for us on meatless Fridays. Over the years, I've added capers and mushrooms to the original recipe but you needn't if you prefer otherwise. Cheese, however, should not be served with this sauce. Its strong flavors will overpower those of the tuna.

INGREDIENTS

3 TBS olive oil
1 medium onion, chopped
3 TBS fresh parsley, chopped
3 cloves garlic, minced
4 to 6 button or crimini mushrooms,
     sliced — optional
2 TBS tomato paste

1 can (28 oz) tomatoes (use crushed,
     diced, or whole that you mash
     during cooking)
1 can (5 oz) of chunk albacore tuna,
     water-packed, well-drained
2 TBS + 1 tsp fresh basil, chopped
3 TBS capers, drained — optional
salt & pepper, to taste

DIRECTIONS

Add oil to a medium sauce pan and heat over a med-high heat. Add onion, garlic, and parsley and sauté until onions are translucent, about 5 minutes.

If using mushrooms, add them now and continue sautéing another 3 or 4 minutes.

Add tomato paste and sauté for about 2 more minutes.

Add tomatoes, stir to thoroughly combine, bring to boil, and reduce to a simmer.

After 30 minutes, carefully add tuna so that the chunks do not fall apart.

Add 2 TBS basil (and capers, if used) to the sauce and stir carefully.

Combine with you favorite cooked pasta and garnish with remaining basil. Serve immediately.

GORGONZOLA SAUCE

Having been served gnocchi with gorgonzola sauce countless times, I decided to recreate the recipe at home. The result is a simple dish that's packed with flavor.

INGREDIENTS

5 oz gorgonzola, crumbled, more or less to taste
½ cup heavy cream, more or less to taste
salt and pepper
grated Pecorino Romano cheese for garnish -- Parmigiano Reggiano may be
*   substituted*
1 lb gnocchi or pasta, cooked and drained
reserved pasta cooking water -- optional

DIRECTIONS

Heat the cream in a small sauce pan over medium heat.

Once the cream is hot, add the gorgonzola and stir until melted.

Taste and adjust, adding more cream or gorgonzola to suit your own taste. If you prefer, you can add a bit of the water used to cook the pasta/gnocchi to thin the sauce without adding more cream.

Don't forget to taste and season with salt & pepper, if required.

Use to dress the gnocchi or pasta. Stir to evenly coat.

.

Serve immediately, garnished with grated cheese.

Note: For something a little different, dress the gnocchi with the gorgonzola sauce and place in an oven-proof dish. Sprinkle the top with bread crumbs that have been mixed with a little melted butter. Place the baking dish in a pre-heated 400° oven and bake until the topping begins to color, about 5 to 10 minutes.

PENNE WITH VODKA SAUCE

Basically, this is nothing more than a tomato sauce laced with cream and vodka. It really is that simple. Over the years, what began as a meatless dish has evolved and I now make it using prosciutto, although I have been known to serve it using ham, pancetta or even shrimp. You can pretty much use whatever protein you want and about the only thing you cannot skip is the vodka. Do that and all you've got is a tomato sauce with some cream.

When cooking with vodka or any alcoholic beverage, I use a brand that I would normally drink.

Note: Be sure to have the pot's lid handy before you add the vodka to the hot pan. Should the vodka ignite, the lid can be used to quickly extinguish the flames.

INGREDIENTS

olive oil
1 TBS butter
¼ to ⅓ lb. chopped prosciutto, cooked ham, or pancetta (optional for vegetarians)
¼ to ½ tsp red pepper flakes, (optional)
1 medium onion, chopped
2 cloves garlic, minced
⅔ cup vodka

1 large (28 oz.) can tomatoes, diced or crushed
½ cup heavy cream
3 TBS fresh parsley, chopped
2 TBS fresh basil, chopped
salt & pepper, to taste
1 lb penne pasta
reserved pasta water
grated Pecorino Romano cheese

DIRECTIONS

Heat oil in a large, deep skillet over med-low heat.

Add pork product and slowly render the fat. Do not cook until crisp.

Increase heat to med-high. Add butter, then onion, and sauté until soft, about 5 minutes. If needed, add some olive oil.

Add the optional red pepper flakes.

Season with salt & pepper, add the garlic, and continue sautéing for another minute

Remove pan from heat, add vodka, stir to combine, return to heat. Have a pan lid nearby to smother the flame should the vodka ignite. Allow to reduce for about 3 minutes.

Add tomatoes, cream, parsley, and stir thoroughly. Bring to a boil, and reduce heat to a low simmer.

After sauce has simmered for 20 minutes, begin heating a large pot of salted water in which to cook the penne. Cook the pasta per package directions, cooking until about 2 minutes before al dente.

Reserving a cup of the pasta water, strain the penne and add the pasta to the tomato sauce.

Continue cooking the combined pasta and sauce until the pasta is done to your liking. Add some of the reserved pasta water to the pan if the pasta becomes dry during this last step of the cooking process.

Just before serving, taste to see if salt or pepper is needed, add the basil, mix well, and garnish the serving platter with grated Pecorino Romano cheese.

Serve immediately.

GRANDPA

Grandpa Bart (LR) and his Family

A BLANK CANVAS

By any measure, the Great Depression hit our family quite hard. Grandpa struggled to keep his family together with a roof over their heads. Even once they married, his daughters remained very close, much to his delight. When an opportunity to purchase the two-flat — once the parish convent — was presented, both families jumped at the chance. We moved into the building in 1956 and Grandpa could not have been more pleased.

It's hard to believe how different the place — more specifically, the back yard — looked when we first arrived. In the back corner of the yard was a rose garden and the rest was, for Grandpa, a blank canvas. He began innocently enough, building a barbecue. We still joke that it would be the only structure in Detroit to survive a

nuclear attack. Not long after that, Grandpa assembled his contractor friends and his garage was built. He had the foresight to attach a patio to one side that was large enough to accommodate both families and several guests for dinner on warm summer evenings, weather permitting. When a neighbor replaced his home's windows, Grandpa grabbed the old windows and hung them on the patio, making it suitable for dining, rain or shine -- so long as you didn't mind running back to the house for supplies in the rain.

Behind the barbecue, he built a dog kennel. He and Dad were hunters and they were forever searching for "that" dog, the perfect pointer/retriever. Inevitably, the dog wasn't suitable and it ended up living the good life out at Cook's farm instead. Eventually, Grandpa converted the kennel into a bird coop, where he kept 2 pairs of Chinese Pheasants. His luck with these exotic birds wasn't much better than he had with the dogs. Although they laid plenty of eggs, none hatched, even after he started transporting them to a friend's incubator.

It was about this time that Grandpa's first garden appeared. Honestly, I do not recall where it was, for those memories have been long crowded out by those of events that were to come, as you'll soon see. At some point, he poured a slab of concrete in front of the patio and shaded it with a grape arbor. He spent many a summer's afternoon reclining in his hammock under that arbor, watering his garden as he listened to his beloved Tigers announced by George Kell. A beer was never beyond his reach.

Bit by bit, our once huge yard was disappearing. Mom, in a rare act of defiance, decided enough was enough and wrote "The End" in a corner of the concrete slab just described. The battle lines were drawn.

A GARDEN NEEDS CARE ...
AND A LITTLE SOUP

Grandpa was very well-read, a trait he used to his advantage when he planned his garden every winter. He studied the Farmer's Almanac and scheduled his planting around the spring lunar calendar. Nothing was left to chance. When the time was right, Grandpa planted his tomatoes using seeds he'd harvested from the prior season's largest tomato and healthiest plant. This is when things got interesting.

It was about this time of the year when Grandpa would corral one of us boys to help him prepare the garden for planting. This meant tilling the earth from one end of the garden to the other. That was the easy part. You see, Grandpa was a firm believer in the power of manure to grow gigantic tomato plants.

About the time we tilled the garden, Grandpa would ask if anyone wanted to go to Cook's farm with him. Cook was a long-time friend of Grandpa and how we kids loved going there! After all, this was the same farm that had adopted our gun-shy hunting dogs, although they were always out running in the fields when we came for a visit. Well, by the time we were old enough to till the garden, the jig was up as far as the dog tales were concerned. We knew full well why we were heading out to Cook's farm on this trip.

(continued)

The fact was that the garden needed manure and not just any manure. Grandpa's tomato crop depended upon this farm's sheep manure. So, once each spring, we drove out to the farm and, after the exchange of a few pleasantries, we drove home with a large metal tub of sheep manure in the trunk, making us very popular at traffic lights if the wind shifted just the right way. Once home, we hauled the tub to the yard but it didn't end there. Oh, if only it ended there!

Grandpa with Cookie

As it turns out, sheep manure, in its natural state, is too strong for young tomato plants and, even if it wasn't, there was no way we could haul enough manure in a car's trunk to cover Grandpa's ever-expanding garden. Grandpa had a solution, all right, and it's lucky that he was so loved by our neighbors. Using a very large metallic bucket and a hose, Grandpa made "soup" — his label not mine — which was then spread over the tilled earth. A couple of days later, one of us would be called upon to till the garden again. Don't think we didn't try to avoid that call to action but we were on our own. Our parents had their eyes on the prize: a wealth of tomatoes come August. Any inkling that we didn't want to help Grandpa was met with a stern reminder that "work never hurt anyone" and suddenly we found ourselves helping Grandpa.

All facts considered, it was only one bad afternoon, leaving 364 pretty good ones. Thankfully, it was early enough in the year that the spring rains helped to quite literally clear the air, much to everyone's relief. Most fortunately, since the boys' bedrooms were closest to the garden, rain and cold temperatures prevented anyone from even considering opening a window to let in some fresh air. And the tomatoes? Grandpa's plants were huge. He used our cracked hockey sticks to support them and the crop was large enough to fulfill the needs of 2 families. Sheep manure soup. Who knew?

SURF AND TURF WARS

With the garden planted and everyone pitching in to help Grandpa complete the summer's big job(s), it looked to outsiders that the two-flat was humming along. No one could have guessed that there was a battle brewing and it rivaled the Old West's grazing wars between the famers and cattle men.

Bill, Ron, Marina,   Rick, and Me

Grandpa wanted to expand his garden, but our first "real" swimming pool — a wire-encircled affair that was about two feet deep — literally stood in his garden's path. Even so, he would never do anything to disappoint his adoring grandchildren. No, not Grandpa. His was a problem that would have befuddled Solomon. You can well imagine, therefore, Grandpa's relief the morning we kids awoke to find that our pool had been completely drained. Upon close examination, we saw that one side of it was inexplicably peppered with holes. While Grandpa, my brother Paul recalls, claimed that some neighborhood kids were to blame, the most attentive among us claimed to have overheard our parents whispering something about buckshot.

Our parents, calmly and coolly, bought and assembled a larger pool. With walls made of corrugated steel, this pool's waters glistened just to the West of the where its predecessor once stood. Grandpa got the room he wanted to expand his garden and we kids had a new, buckshot-proof, pool in which to swim. Life was good — until the discovery that ripening beefsteak tomatoes can somehow attract errant pool toys, especially whenever Grandpa strolled through the yard. If it wasn't a badly thrown beach ball knocking the plants, it was overly enthusiastic splashing drenching them with chlorinated water. Grandpa was not happy.

(continued)

The situation remained unchanged for a couple of summers. Then one morning, we awoke to once again find the backyard flooded and the pool drained. On one side of the pool, in the corrugated steel, was a gash not quite a foot long. Bent inward, the steel pierced the pool's lining and flooded the yard. Depending upon which parent asked, Grandpa replied that my cousin Rick or I did it with the lawn mower. In our defense, I will merely point out that an old push mower was used to maintain the lawns. Even if we teamed up, together pushing that relic and with a 100 foot running start, never could we two young boys get up enough steam to create so much as a dent, let alone pierce, that steel siding. Our wise parents, though they never determined "the how", quickly surmised "the who" and soon thereafter we were erecting a bigger, better, and even sturdier swimming pool. It remained in our yard until it died of natural causes, some years later. All that time, Grandpa stood guard in his garden making sure that his tomato plants got the respect they deserved.

WHEN THERE'S A JOB TO BE DONE

When he wasn't working in the garden or patrolling the "shore" looking for errant beach balls, one would think that Grandpa could sit back and relax. Yes, one would think.

The Two-Flat (c 1959)

Grandpa was, by all accounts, a Jack-of-all-Trades. Having owned a contracting business, few maintenance and repair jobs around the old two-flat fell outside of his skill set. At any given time, especially in the summer, he could usually be found performing any one of a number of jobs around the building: cement work, carpentry, tile setting, painting, roof repair, and the occasional electrical project. Once, we came home to see a patch of fresh tar on the roof. While we were away, Grandpa got up on the roof and patched it. Another time he corralled The Max Whisperer into helping him "adjust" the back of the house. With no basement to support that part of the building, it was sinking, ever so slowly. Grandpa and cousin Ron got into the claustrophobic crawl space and, using four huge jacks, gave the house the support it needed. Another summer, he summoned the in-house work crew to strip the shingles that covered the exterior of the second floor, replacing them with stucco.

As children, we were often enlisted to help him with these projects. When very little, our main duty was to stay out of the way. We soon graduated to beer fetchers and water bearers. "Go-fer" was the next position and, depending on the project and number of men involved, we could be kept running, fetching tools, bricks, you name it. Soon we were allowed to water the dry ingredients to make cement, under supervision of course. Not long thereafter, we were permitted to use the two-hole hoe to mix the cement, as well as a variety of small jobs. You might, for example, fill buckets with cement, haul them, maybe cut a board or two, hammer a few nails, etc. And then, one day, you were deemed old enough and big enough to push a loaded wheelbarrow. That was the pinnacle of success for us laborers, for it meant that we were capable of doing man's work. Make no mistake, pushing a wheelbarrow full of cement was certainly man's work, especially under the watchful eyes of the adults present. You did not want to tip a full wheel barrow in front of that audience. There were plenty of opportunities, too, because there was at least one job every summer that required cement. After Mom wrote "The End" in that cement slab, cement jobs grew scarce, but that didn't mean Grandpa was finished. No, there was still work to be done and sometimes Grandpa flew solo, like the time he painted the trim of the house.

Unlike bungalows and ranch-style homes, painting a two-flat's trim was no easy task. Much of the trim was about 25 feet above the ground, with the peak another 8 or so feet higher. To further complicate matters, there were 2 aluminum awnings attached to the front of the house, a small one over Zia's living room window, while a much larger awning shielded our first floor windows and the entire porch, minus the building's entryway. When Grandpa decided the trim needed painting, he was about 71 years of age. This was long before "70 is the new 50"; 70 was 70 and I was about 15.

The Two-Flat 25 Years After We Left (c 2010)

One summer afternoon, Grandpa called for me to give him a hand. By the time I got to the front of the house, Grandpa had already started up the ladder and was waiting for me. The ladder, however, was not long enough to reach the top, or even near the top, of the peak. Not only that but the awnings prevented it from resting against the building. Instead, it was on a bit of an incline as it laid across both awnings, its top-end suspended a little more than a foot from the wall.

(continued)

When he saw me, I was instructed to stand on the bottom of the ladder. Grandpa then began to climb higher. In his hand was a hockey stick with a paint brush lashed to the end. I started pleading with him to stop. He ignored me and further up he went. I didn't know it, but he had already placed a bucket of paint on top of the first awning. When he reached the end of the ladder, and with his left arm acting as a brace against the side of the building, he started painting the building's peak, dipping his hockey stick brush into the paint can below him and then swinging it over his head. Whether because he heard my voice or just by luck, a neighbor came out and, horrified, ran to help me steady the ladder, all the while yelling, "Bart, get down!" Grandpa, of course, ignored him, as well. There was a job to be done, after all. Within minutes, a few more neighbors came, all pleading with him to stop. All for naught. The parish school was across the street and at the end of the block. At the time, Mom worked there as the school's secretary. That day, being it was summer, Mom left her office at 4:00 pm.

She didn't walk far before she noticed the gathering on our lawn and quickened her pace. When she got close enough, she noticed Grandpa on the ladder, swinging a hockey stick. Now running, and a few doors away, Mom was yelling, "Pa! Get Down!" Unperturbed, Grandpa kept painting.

When he had finished, the entire episode having lasted no more than 30 minutes, Grandpa calmly came down the ladder, handed his hockey stick to someone, went back up for the paint can, and came back down again for the last time. Mom and the neighbors demanded that he stop painting and he complied. In reality, his compliance was by no means submission. The peak was the last of the trim to be painted. His work was done.

The men helped Grandpa put away the ladder and paint supplies. For that, he invited them back to "see my tomatoes." These invitations, however, had very little to do with tomatoes.

WOULD YOU LIKE TO SEE MY TOMATOES?

Once summer arrived, with the garden planted and the season's chores well underway, if not completed, Grandpa had time to relax a bit. On warm days, you might find him relaxing in his hammock listening to a Tiger baseball game. After the game, or when there was no game, Grandpa often went for a stroll.

Well-known throughout the neighborhood, all were accustomed to seeing him out and about. If he heard the rumble of heavy equipment or the whirr of power tools, he would be at the job site or backyard within minutes. With his contracting background, Grandpa knew and understood quite a bit about building and repair work. It wouldn't be long before he'd be advising the worker(s) and oftentimes he'd pitch in, showing them how whatever it was should be done. His opinion was respected and very often sought by our neighbors. Nothing pleased him more.

It wasn't just our neighbors who enlisted his help. When lightning struck the parish school, it was Grandpa they asked to repair the masonry. The front of our church, built about 1960, was a massive, floor-to-ceiling mosaic depicting a number of saints and religious symbols. As the church settled, a large crack began to appear in the center of the mosaic at its base, stretching upward like some leafless tree. Grandpa was called upon to repair the crack, replacing the many tiny colored tiles.

To be sure, there were plenty of afternoons when Grandpa's stroll was just that, a walk around the neighborhood, stopping to chat with whoever he met. It didn't matter who you were — neighbor, parish priest, mail carrier, passer-by, etc. — if Grandpa saw you, he would strike up a conversation and, at just the right moment, invite you to "see my tomatoes." Within minutes, there you were, looking at his 2 dozen tomato plants, tied to their hockey sticks in neat little rows. He'd show you the brick barbecue, his very much prized Chinese pheasants, the lettuce patch, the grape vines, the potted lemon tree, and his latest attempt at growing a fig tree. Within minutes you'd be invited into the patio, and he'd have a cold one in front of you before you had settled into your chair. What's this? You don't like beer? Not to worry. There was a jug of red wine under the table. Oh?

(continued)

You prefer white wine? There just so happened to be a jug of white wine next to the red.

Well, that first beer or glass of wine led to another and another and then another. Somewhere along the line, shot glasses would appear and whiskey was introduced into the conversation. Although the length of these backyard tours varied, they usually ended in the same way, with his guest leaving the yard quite a bit more wobbly than when the tour first began. In fact, there were a few times when one of us kids was asked to walk his guest home. These visits did not go unnoticed by the wives in the neighborhood, and a few men refused Grandpa's subsequent invitations. Others would accept but leave abruptly after the first beer. Of course, there were those who accepted the invitation with no qualms at all. It was after one such visit that a neighbor approached Mom, angry because her husband had ignored her wishes and had returned home mom ents before, more wobbly than usual. I don't recall whether she wanted Mom to control Grandpa, her husband, or both, but Mom, recognizing a no win situation, did nothing of the kind. The husband, perhaps wisely, kept his distance, and I don't recall ever seeing him in the backyard again. That's too bad because he missed one of the greatest parties ever held in our yard.

It was Grandpa's birthday, though neither Zia nor I can remember the exact one. As was the case for each of his birthdays, all 12 of us ate dinner together on the patio, with a couple of family friends seated at the table, as well. Once the dinner was finished, neighbors and friends joined the party just in time for cake and liquid refreshments. As I said, Grandpa was well-known and you never really knew who'd show up. This year, even the parish Pastor stopped by. The poor man didn't stand a chance for the wine, beer, and whiskey flowed freely.

I've no idea how much time had transpired but I do know that my Dad was seated on our front porch as Grandpa walked the priest back to his rectory located at the other end of our block. Dad was still on the porch when the two returned a while later. Apparently, when they finally reached the rectory, the priest kindly offered to walk Grandpa home. He accepted, and so they returned. Realizing that this could go on for hours, Dad offered to walk the good priest home and sent Grandpa to bed. Oddly enough, although he was invited, our Pastor was a no-show at Grandpa's next birthday party. That was OK, however, for another priest, a recent transfer from Wisconsin, happily took his place ... like a lamb to the slaughter.

At long last, retired

FIRST COURSES
PRIMI PIATTI

Mom with Dad, Home On Leave

GRANDMAS' GARBANZO SOUP
MINESTRA DI CECI

Whether you call them garbanzos, chickpeas, or *ceci*, this bean is a good one to have in your pantry. Very low in fat and high in protein, garbanzos are becoming more popular as gluten-free and vegetarian diets become more common. When ground, the resulting flour is a viable substitute for gluten flours. Most readily available dried or in cans, garbanzos can be used in any number of ways. In a country where meat was once reserved for special occasions, garbanzos were one of several beans Italians used to supply protein to their diets.

Grandma Erselia, Mom and Zia's Mother, prepared this soup on Christmas Eve as did Nonna. Being meatless, it followed the Church's abstinence laws for the day before Christmas. As is the case with most of the Bartolini recipes from back in the day, this soup is simple to prepare and relies on a few, commonplace ingredients. As you can imagine, the most important thing you'll put in your stockpot is the stock itself. Though the recipe here uses a vegetable stock, feel free to use whatever type of stock you prefer.

INGREDIENTS

2 cups dried garbanzo beans/chickpeas, inspected to remove stones and the like
2 quarts vegetable stock
1 onion, chopped

1 TBS butter
1 TBS olive oil
salt & pepper to taste
grated Pecorino Romano cheese for serving

DIRECTIONS

At least 8 hours or the night before, place the beans in a large bowl and cover with water that is at least 2 inches above the beans. Before use, pour off the water, rinse, and set aside to drain. Do not allow to dry out. No need to soak canned beans. Just rinse and proceed.

Heat the oil and butter in a large, heavy-bottomed pot over med-high heat. Add the onion and sauté until translucent — about 5 minutes. Do not allow it to brown. Season lightly with salt and pepper.

Add the stock and chickpeas to the pot and stir. Bring to a boil before reducing to a simmer.

Continue to simmer until the beans are as tender as you like.

Check for seasoning before serving with plenty of grated cheese at the table.

Note: If using canned garbanzo beans, one cup dried equals about two 15 oz cans.

TRENETTE WITH SOFT SHELL CRAB AND MOREL MUSHROOMS

It wasn't all that long ago that I discovered a fishmonger not far from my home. Not only do they pride themselves in offering sustainable seafood but they offer a variety of other items, too. Farm fresh eggs, ramps, mushrooms, and a fine olive oil are just a few of the items they have on-hand. When their newsletter announced they had both soft shell crabs and morel mushrooms in supply, I wasted no time and placed an order. This pasta is the dish I served that evening.

INGREDIENTS

1 lb trenette - linguine may be used
3 or 4 soft shelled crabs, cleaned (your fishmonger will prepare them)
2 TBS butter
2 TBS olive oil
3 cloves garlic, smashed
red pepper flakes, to taste
2 to 4 oz morel mushrooms, halved
salt & pepper to taste
pasta water
fresh parsley, for garnish

DIRECTIONS

Heat oil and butter in a large frypan over medium heat. Add the garlic and sauté until garlic is browned but not burned. Discard garlic, leaving the oil in the pan.

Add the red pepper flakes and soft shell crabs to the pan, lower the heat to med-low, and cover.

Continue to sauté gently for about 10 minutes, turning them over midway through.

Meanwhile, bring to the boil a 6 to 8 quart pot of water. Add 1 TBS salt and the trenette. Cook until the pasta is about 2 minutes shy of al dente. Time it so that both pasta and crabs are ready at the same time. Be sure to reserve some pasta water.

Add the morels to the frypan, drain the trenette, and add it to the frypan, too. Stir to coat the pasta with the oil.

Continue to cook until the pasta is done to your liking. Add some of the reserved pasta water, as needed.

Serve immediately, garnished with chopped fresh parsley.

Note: Trenette is a pasta that comes from Liguria, Slightly thinner than linguine, I like it because it most closely resembles the pasta that Mom and Zia hand-cut when I was young. Luckily, my machine has an attachment that creates this pasta.

MOM'S SPLIT PEA SOUP

INGREDIENTS

FOR THE HAM STOCK

1 ham bone, some meat left on
2 partially cooked, smoked ham
    hocks
2 onions, quartered
4 carrots, quartered
4 celery stalks leaves attached,
    quartered
parsley stems
2 bay leaves
4 quarts water

FOR THE PEA SOUP

2 lb dried split peas
3 to 4 quarts ham stock
3 or 4 carrots, diced or sliced, as
    preferred
8 oz roasted ham, cubed — more or less,
    to taste
ham removed from bone, trimmed &
    chopped
meat from ham hocks, trimmed &
    chopped
salt & pepper, to taste
croutons for serving

DIRECTIONS

FOR THE HAM STOCK

Put all the stock's ingredients into a large, heavy bottomed pot, bring to a boil, and then reduce to a low simmer.

Continue to simmer for 2 hours, skimming surface foam occasionally, as needed.

After 2 hours, remove meat from pot and reserve. Pour stock through a fine mesh sieve or clean kitchen towel to remove remaining vegetables and other bits, resulting in a clean stock. Reserve.

When cool enough to handle, trim the meat from the bones and chop into bite-sized pieces. Cover and reserve.

FOR THE PEA SOUP

Add all the soup's ingredients to a slow cooker. If you did not create enough stock in the previous step, add water to augment.

Set on "low" and cook for 8 hours or set on "high" and cook for 4 hours.

Check for seasoning and serve garnished with croutons.

As much as she enjoyed split pea soup, Mom rarely prepared it. As I recall, Mom and I were the only ones who enjoyed the soup. The others, at best, endured it. Not only that but we rarely had baked ham for dinner. Our holiday meals were pretty much tradition and ham just didn't make the cut. Besides, I don't think that Dad was at all interested in baked ham, since I cannot remember it ever being served on a Sunday or any other night that Dad was home for dinner. So, with ham being served so rarely, there were no ham leftovers and, consequently, no split pea soup. I know my vegan and vegetarian friends will take issue with what I'm about to write but here it is. You must have ham to make good split pea soup. Mom said so.

Mom with Pookie

Though it's true that we might not have had it often, Mom and I still did enjoy our split pea soup. She usually served it when it was just the two of us for lunch and it became something of a special treat. Later, after I moved away, whenever I told her that I was going to bake a ham — or had just done so — she would ask if I was going to make split pea soup, asking for each and every detail of the recipe. And more than once I brought a frozen ham bone home to Michigan with me, made a pot of split pea soup, and left it for her safely stored in her freezer. Today, I'll often bake a ham for Easter and save the bone. On Mother's Day, I still make Mom's favorite soup.

PASSATINI SOUP

Let me start by stating that when I was a boy, my Mom was the coolest Mom on the block. After I'd spent the morning hard at play, manufacturing Creepy Crawlers with my Mattel Thingmaker©, guess what she served for lunch? Worms. That's right, WORMS! How cool was that? Granted, we didn't have actual worms for lunch but we did have passatini, a far more appetizing and tasty alternative. Sometimes called *passatelli*, passatini are noodles, of a sort, made with bread crumbs and cheese instead of flour and lightly flavored with lemon zest and nutmeg. The noodles are extruded using a special press, a large-holed ricer, or a meat grinder. Once made, they can be added immediately to a pot of boiling stock or placed in single layers on baking sheets to be frozen. After a couple of hours, the now frozen passatini may be gently placed into a container and stored in an area of the freezer where they won't be disturbed. As you may have guessed, these noodles are more delicate than most and care needs to be taken when storing them. On the other hand, this recipe can be halved easily, thereby eliminating the need for freezing altogether. Whether freshly made or previously frozen, a steaming bowl of passatini is a meal fit for the coldest of winter's days. And if you happen to be serving children of a certain age, you, too, can be as cool as my Mom.

INGREDIENTS

2 cups bread crumbs
1 to 1½ cups grated Pecorino Romano or
    Parmigiano cheese
½ TBS lemon zest

½ tsp ground nutmeg
4 large eggs
chicken stock (p 19)
grated cheese for serving

DIRECTIONS

Combine lemon zest with dry ingredients in a large bowl.

Add eggs and mix until a dough is formed. (I use my stand mixer and paddle attachment.)

Form into a ball, cover, and let dough rest for 10 minutes.

Using a large-holed potato ricer or meat grinder plate, extrude the passatini and place in a single layer on baking sheets, to be used immediately or frozen for later use.

Bring a pot of stock to boil, add the passatini, and reduce to a medium simmer. Cook for three additional minutes after the passatini begin to float and serve with grated cheese on the side.

PEPPER AND CHEESE PASTA
CACIO E PEPE

There is a surprising number of pasta recipes with very few ingredients and this is one of them. As a young adult, living on my own with a bare cupboard, Cacio e Pepe was my Ramen noodles, quick to prepare and cheap. Although my situation is far different today, I make this dish often and, when I do, I cannot help but think of Zia's husband, Uncle Al, when I catch a whiff of this dish's aroma.

Living in the two-flat, there were many dinners where the families ate together and very often some form of pasta was served. My Uncle, like most, enjoyed grated cheese atop his pasta but what set his plate apart from everyone else's was his love of black pepper. To my eye, he used more pepper than anyone seated at the table. Well, for this youngster, the aroma of grated Pecorino Romano mingling with the scent of freshly cracked pepper was intoxicating, made even more so because I was considered too young to have access to the pepper shaker. I eventually grew up, as most young boys tend to do, and was finally able to add as much pepper to my pasta as I wanted -- and I did and still do, for that matter.

INGREDIENTS

1 TBS salt
your favorite pasta - spaghetti,
linguine, capellini, etc.
freshly cracked pepper

freshly grated Pecorino Romano
cheese - Parmigiano may be
substituted
reserved pasta cooking water

DIRECTIONS

Bring a 6 to 8 quart pot of water to boil before adding the salt and your favorite pasta.

Towards the end of the pasta's cooking, warm the serving platter by running very hot water over it.

When al dente, drain the pasta, reserving some of the pasta water as you do. It's best if you do not fully drain the pasta.

Place the pasta in the warmed serving bowl, add plenty of grated cheese, and stir to combine, adding some pasta water to make a sauce, of sorts.

Season heavily with freshly cracked pepper and serve immediately.

LINGUINE WITH CLAMS
LINGUINE CON LE VONGOLE

When in Italy, I make sure to enjoy a plate of linguine with clams at least once while I'm there. They've clams unlike any available here, so very sweet. Even so, our clams are worthy substitutes and I'll gladly use them when I've a taste for this pasta dish.

The recipe is easy enough but totally time dependent. You'll want your pasta to be ready just as the clams open up. Miss-time the dish's parts and your pasta may be over-cooked or clams rubbery.

Note: Today, clams bought at your grocery may not need more cleaning than as indicated in the recipe. If you've harvested your own clams or bought some along the shore, you should repeat the soaking step outlined a few times more than specified.

INGREDIENTS

at least 2 doz. little neck or manila
    clams
3 TBS olive oil
1 to 2 cloves of garlic, minced
3 TBS fresh parsley, chopped¼ cup
white wine or water

salt & pepper, to taste
1 TBS salt
1 lb linguine - fettuccine, or tagliatelle
    may be substituted
chopped parsley for garnish

DIRECTIONS

At least an hour before dinner, use a brush to individually scrub each clam before rinsing and placing it in a large bowl of cold freshwater. Discard any clams with broken shells or that do not close tightly when scrubbed. Change the water at least once before proceeding with the recipe.

Bring a 6 to 8 quart pot of water to boil. Add 1 TBS salt.

Add oil to a large frying pan with a lid. Add the garlic, parsley and the wine or water.

Add the pasta to the pot of salted boiling water. The pasta, if dried, should take 9 or 10 minutes to cook. If fresh, less time will be needed. Time it so that its completion coincides with that of the clams.

Just when the frying pan's liquid begins to show signs of boiling, add the clams and cover tightly,

In about 5 to 8 minutes, the clams should be open & steamed. Discard any unopened clams. Replace cover and remove from heat.

Reserve 1 cup of the pasta water, drain the pasta, and combine the clams & pan juices with the drained pasta. If too dry, add some of the reserved pasta water.

Serve immediately, garnished with chopped parsley.

Please do not use cheese with this dish. Its delicate flavors will disappear when the stronger tasting cheese is added.

PLAIN OR WHITE PASTA
PASTA IN BIANCO

Pasta in bianco, also called pasta bianco, is a pasta dish served plain without sauce. It's about as simple a pasta dish as one can make. When I was a boy, Mom would serve this to me whenever I was recuperating from some sort of stomach ailment. I always thought that this "cure" was something peculiar to our house and it wasn't until many years later that I learned that many Italian households do the same. Luckily, one doesn't need to be ill to enjoy this simple, yet surprisingly flavorful, dish. Requiring so few ingredients, this can easily be your "go to" dinner if you want something to eat but don't have the time nor desire to cook a "normal" meal.

INGREDIENTS

1 TBS salt
½ lb angel hair/capellini or spaghetti
     or linguine
4 TBS butter
¼ cup Pecorino Romano cheese -
     may be substituted
pepper, to taste
reserved pasta cooking water

DIRECTIONS

Fill a large 6 to 8 quart pot with water and bring to a rolling boil.

Add the salt, then the pasta, and stir to help prevent the pasta from sticking.

Follow package directions and cook the pasta, stirring occasionally, until al dente. Drain the pasta, reserving a cup of the pasta water in the proces. Do NOT rinse with cold water.

Return pasta to the pot, add butter, and stir to evenly coat. Add cheese and mix well. Add a little of the reserved pasta water, if too dry.

Serve immediately. Have additional cheese and freshly ground pepper available at the table.

STRACCIATELLA SOUP

Stracciatella is an Italian egg drop soup that is common to San Marino and Marche, as well as the Lazio and Emilia-Romagna regions The name is derived from the Italian word that means "torn apart" or "rags" and that's an apt description for the dish. The eggs look like tiny torn rags in the broth. A tasty soup, this easy-to-prepare dish makes a perfect lunch or first course.

INGREDIENTS

3 large eggs
¼ cup grated Parmigiano Reggiano
    cheese
1 TBS fresh parsley, chopped
a pinch of freshly ground nutmeg

8 cups (2 quarts) chicken stock (p 19)
    (vegetable stock may be
    substituted)
salt & pepper, to taste
grated parmesan cheese for serving

DIRECTIONS

Combine eggs, cheese, parsley, and nutmeg in a bowl or container with a pouring spout and mix well.

Place stock into a sauce pan and heat over a med-high heat.

When it begins to boil, reduce heat to medium-low. With one hand, use a spoon to gently stir the stock in a circular motion and, with the other hand, slowly pour the egg mixture into the pan.

When all the egg mixture has been added, stop stirring and continue simmering for another minute or so.

Taste the soup and season with salt & pepper, if needed.

Serve immediately with additional grated parmesan cheese.

Note: Many will add a bit of cooked chopped spinach to the soup, once the egg has been added and cooked. Although strictly speaking, this is not stracciatella soup, it is a very tasty version, nonetheless.

PASTA WITH GARLIC AND OIL
AGLIO E OLIO

As a young adult still living in the two-flat, I'd come home after a night out with the boys and, while they were in a drive-thru waiting for their sack o' sliders, I was already fixing myself a plate of aglio e olio. One of those nights, as I was eating, Uncle Al came down the back stairs to see what I was cooking. After a brief chat, he went back upstairs. A week or two later, the same thing happened but, this time, he mentioned how quickly I had prepared the dish. Realizing the implication, I was ready for him the next time. A couple of weeks later, after a night spent carousing with friends, I set out to make my late night dinner, only this time I slowed things down a bit. Sure enough, Uncle appeared but this time I was just about to add the pasta to the boiling water (*butta giù* in our house's parlance). I added enough spaghetti for two and within minutes we were enjoying a late night snack together. We dined together several times after that and I always knew that if he didn't appear by the time I was ready to butta giù, I would be dining alone. To this day, I cannot have a dish of pasta aglio e olio without thinking of those late night dinners together.

Throughout the years, this simple dish has continued to serve me well. After a long day at work or on those evenings I didn't feel much like cooking, I could easily prepare this pasta in a fraction of the time it would take to have a dinner delivered. Best of all, I still find it every bit as satisfying as I did those many years ago, although, admittedly, my dog Max is hardly the conversationalist that Uncle Al was.

INGREDIENTS

1 TBS salt

1 lb spaghetti (cappellini, spaghettini, linguine, or trenette may be used)

½ cup extra virgin olive oil

½ to 1 tsp red pepper flakes or 1 red peperoncino, diced - optional

3 to 6 cloves of garlic, diced

reserved pasta water

½ cup grated Pecorino Romano cheese – Parmigiano Reggiano may be substituted - separated

chopped parsley, for garnish - optional

grated cheese for serving - optional

DIRECTIONS

Bring a 6 to 8 quart pot of water to boil. Add the salt and spaghetti and stir.

Check the spaghetti package's cooking instructions. About 3 minutes before the spaghetti is supposed to be cooked al dente, begin heating the oil in a deep frying pan.

Add the pepper flakes (or peperoncino) & garlic and sauté until the edges of the garlic just begin to turn brown, no more than 2 minutes. Do not allow the garlic to brown completely or, worse yet, to burn. Your pasta should be ready about now.

Reserve 1 cup of the pasta water, strain the pasta, add it to the frying pan, and stir to combine and to coat the pasta.

Add a few ounces of the reserved pasta water to the pan with the pasta, more as needed. Allow the pasta to finish cooking, to your liking.

Before serving, take the pan off of the heat, add all but 2 TBS of the cheese, and mix until well-coated. Garnish with parsley and the remaining cheese.

Serve immediately.

STRAW AND HAY PASTA
PAGLIA E FIENO

So named because its green and yellow noodles resemble straw and hay, *paglia e fieno* was a favorite of both families in the two-flat every spring. Unlike today, frozen foods were just beginning to appear in stores, so, making this dish meant shelling peas. I helped Mom shell them — until I grew up a little and the novelty wore off. After that, I made myself scarce when the metal colander and bag of peas appeared. Still, even once Bird's Eye became a household name, fresh peas continued to be used to make this dish every spring. As good as frozen peas may be, you just cannot beat the taste of fresh. If there's one thing to be said about the best of Italian cooking, it's that it relies upon the freshest of ingredients. To that end, my Zia and I continue to enjoy this dish every spring while, at the home of Rick, her youngest son, it wouldn't be Easter if paglia e fieno isn't served.

INGREDIENTS

1 TBS salt
½ lb yellow fettuccine (linguine,
*   tagliatelle, or pappardelle may*
*   be substituted)*
½ lb green-colored pasta of the same type
*   as the yellow pasta - use a little*
*   chopped spinach to color the*
*   pasta*
3 TBS butter
1 TBS olive oil

1 small onion, chopped fine
3 cloves garlic, minced
1 cup heavy cream
4 to 6 oz prosciutto
1 cup fresh peas
½ cup Pecorino Romano cheese,
*   grated — more for serving*
salt and pepper, to taste
reserved pasta water

DIRECTIONS

Add salt to a 6 to 8 quart pot of boiling water for cooking the pasta.

Time it so that the pasta is just shy of al dente about the time that the peas are cooked to your liking. Reserve 1 cup of the pasta water.

Heat oil and butter in a large, deep frying pan over med-high heat. Add onion and sauté for 2 to 3 minutes.

Add the prosciutto and continue to sauté until the onions are translucent, about an additional 3 to 5 minutes.

Add garlic and continue to cook for another minute.

Add heavy cream and simmer for several minutes until reduced by ⅓. Add the peas, stirring until well-combined. If sauce becomes too thick, add a little pasta water to thin it.

When pasta is just shy of al dente and peas are sufficiently cooked, taste to check seasoning and add the cooked pasta to the frying pan. Stir well. If necessary, add some pasta water to thin the sauce.

Remove from heat, add grated cheese, mix thoroughly, and move to a serving platter.

Serve immediately, garnished with grated cheese, parsley, and cracked pepper.

Note: You can also cook the peas in the pasta water along with the fettuccine. Just remember that fresh pasta requires less time than store bought to be cooked *al dente.*

LASAGNA

Long before my memories begin, Mom and Zia had grown tired of lasagna made with the traditional *besciamella* sauce. The two Sisters put their aprons together and came up with this recipe's cheese sauce that's made with cream cheese. The result is one terrific lasagna, unlike any you've tried before.

INGREDIENTS - LASAGNA

tomato sauce, with/without meat - see
p 16 or 18
enough cooked lasagna noodles (or "No Boil") to make 3 or 4 pasta layers
cheese sauce - recipe follows
an 8 oz ball of fresh mozzarella, - packaged can be substituted
Pecorino Romano cheese, grated

TO MAKE THE CHEESE SAUCE

INGREDIENTS

6 TBS butter
12 oz cream cheese
2 to 3 TBS whole milk

Place butter, cream cheese, and milk in a microwave proof bowl. Microwave on high, for 3 to 4 minutes, depending upon the microwave's power. Alternately, heat the ingredients in a small saucepan over a low heat.

Remove and whisk until smooth. Set aside until needed.

TO ASSEMBLE THE LASAGNA

Pre-heat oven to 350° F and generously butter a baking dish or nonreactive pan.

Coat the bottom of the dish with tomato sauce before adding one layer of noodles.

Coat the noodles with tomato sauce and ⅓ of the cheese sauce. Spread them evenly before sprinkling with grated cheese.

Repeat the prior 2 steps once or twice, depending upon noodles used and the depth of the dish or pan used.

Add a final layer of noodles then cover with the remaining tomato sauce.

Slice the mozzarella and place on top and sprinkle with Pecorino Romano cheese.

Place in pre-heated oven and bake until heated through, 40 yo 45 minutes or until top layer of cheese is cooked to your liking. If using sliced mozzarella, once the lasagna has baked for 45 minutes, raise the oven temperature to 400° F and continue until top layer of cheese is cooked to your liking - about 10 to 15 minutes.

Let rest at least 15 minutes before serving.

Note: Whether you make lasagna following this recipe or your own, I cannot suggest strongly enough that you prepare your own pasta noodles. The dish will be greatly improved.

CANNELLONI

Cannelloni are another of Italy's stuffed pastas, though these are more in the style of *manicotti* rather than *ravioli* or *agnolotti*. As much as we all loved them — we kids called them "cigars" — cannelloni weren't served for dinner very often. Unlike ravioli or cappelletti, which were "assigned" holidays, cannelloni were served when Mom or Zia found the time to make them. Remember, there were no freezers so a cannelloni dinner meant that they would have been up at dawn, rolling out pasta dough. As a result, though it wasn't a holiday, a cannelloni dinner was a special occasion, to be sure.

As for the pasta sheets, roll your dough as thin as you would when making hand-cut pasta. Depending upon the size of your baking dish, cut your dough strip in rectangles about 3 X 4". Remember that the dough will expand a little once par-boiled. (You may wish to boil a test piece to make sure it will fit the dish.) Once the pasta is cut, place the sheets in rapidly boiling, salted water. Cook for no more than 2 minutes if using freshly made pasta. Store-bought will require a few minutes more. Strain the pasta and immediately place in an ice bath to stop the cooking process. At this point the sheets are ready for use. You can either take a few out of the ice water and separate them on to clean, moist towels, and use them one-at-a-time, or take them out of the bath one-at-a-time, pat dry to remove excess water, and use as indicated in the recipe. Either way, using fresh pasta produces a far superior dish to anything you can buy at a store.

INGREDIENTS

FOR THE CANNELLONI

Mom's pasta dough - p 26
cannelloni filling - p 54
1 quart tomato sauce, with or without meat - pp 16 or 18
cheese sauce - recipe follows
an 8 oz ball of fresh mozzarella, - packaged can be substituted
½ cup grated Pecorino Romano cheese

FOR THE CHEESE SAUCE

2 to 3 oz cream cheese, softened
2 to 3 oz milk
2 TBS butter, melted

DIRECTIONS

TO MAKE THE CANNELLONI *(picture to follow)*

Shape 2 to 3 TBS of filling into a small log, about as thick as your index finger. More or less filling may be required depending upon the size of your cannelloni. Do not over-stuff.

Filling should leave a ¼ inch border on either side of the dough sheet.

Place the filling on the edge of the dough sheet and roll as one would if making a cigar.

Set aside, seam-side down.

Repeat the previous steps until all the filling or dough sheets have been used.

(continued)

Note: At this point, the cannelloni may be placed on a baking sheet and placed in the freezer. Once frozen, place in freezer-proof container for use at a later date.

ASSEMBLE THE DISH AND BAKE

Pre-heat oven to 350° F. Liberally butter a baking dish.

Coat the bottom of the dish with about 1 cup of tomato sauce

Place cannelloni, seam side down, in 2 rows, until dish is filled. Do not over-crowd.

Combine the ingredients to make the cheese sauce and spoon over the cannelloni.

Add enough of the remaining tomato sauce to completely cover the dish's contents.

Sprinkle the top with the grated mozzarella and Pecorino Romano cheeses.

Spray one side of a sheet of aluminum foil with cooking spray and use it to cover the baking dish, sprayed side down.

Bake in pre-heated 350° F oven for 20 minutes. Remove foil and continue baking until cheese topping is cooked to your satisfaction. Over-cooking may result in dry cannelloni.

Allow to rest 10 minutes before serving.

SPINACH-RICOTTA STUFFED SHELLS

INGREDIENTS

butter
1 pound fresh ricotta
1 pkg (10 oz) frozen chopped spinach,
    cooked and well-drained
1 cup grated parmesan cheese
2 eggs, slightly beaten
1 tsp kosher salt

⅛ tsp ground nutmeg
1 quart pasta sauce, with or without
    meat - pp 16 or 18
1 box jumbo pasta shells, cooked
    following package directions,
    reserved in cold water.
1 cup grated mozzarella, or more to taste

DIRECTIONS

Pre-heat oven to 350° F. Butter one 9 x 13" baking dish/pan.

Place ricotta, spinach, parmesan cheese, eggs, salt, and nutmeg into a bowl and combine, either by hand or using a stand mixer, until well-blended.

Pour about half of the sauce into the baking dish.

One by one, fill each shell with about 2 TBS of the filling mixture and place in the baking dish.

When the tray is filled, drizzle remaining sauce over the tops of the stuffed shells. Sprinkle with mozzarella and cover with aluminum foil. Spraying the foil with cooking spray may prevent it from sticking to the melted cheese.

Place on oven's center rack and bake for 30 minutes. Remove foil and continue baking for 15 minutes more.

By now you may have noticed that we don't use much ricotta in our recipes. Well, this is the exception that proves the rule. These shells feature ricotta, as well as 2 more cheeses, enough for even the biggest of cheese lovers.

The recipe will make about 24 shells. If that's too much for one dinner, they can easily be frozen for another day. You can assemble the tray, sauce and all, and wrap it well before freezing, or, place the filled shells on baking sheets and put them into a freezer. Once frozen, pack the shells in freezer-proof bags/containers and return to the freezer until needed.

ACINI DI PEPE SOUP WITH MEATBALLS
MINESTRA CON POLPETTINE

This soup came to our family from the mother of my 5th grade teacher. "Mr. D" was from Upstate New York. My class was his first in Detroit, having arrived barely 1 week before school started that September. Mr. D wanted to introduce himself to the parish and to our parents, so, once classes started, he visited the home of each of his students. He chose the families alphabetically, making mine the second home he entered. As was so often the case with newcomers who entered the two-flat, he hung around for a number of years afterward. Eventually, Mr. D migrated upstairs, becoming a good friend of Zia and Uncle Al. At some point, and I do not recall how much time had transpired, his Mother and Aunt came to Detroit for a visit. It wasn't long before they, too, became ensnared in the two-flat's web of conviviality. Well, as luck would have it, both women were good cooks and during subsequent visits, recipes were traded. One of the very few recipes to survive is today's minestra, Acini di Pepe with meatballs.

Resembling peppercorns, Acini di Pepe is a small pasta that expands during the cooking process, much like couscous. Mom served it to Sis when her tummy was upset, just as she served my brother and I quadretti - p 38. As was her way, Doctor Mom started with broth only and gradually added increasing amounts of Acini di Pepe to the broth as Sis's condition improved. The meatballs, *polpettine*, were never used for medicinal purposes. They were served when everyone was well and seated at the dinner table. We sure did enjoy them! The lemon zest in the meatballs, when mixed with a hint of nutmeg, take this simple soup to an entirely different level. Now, if Acini di Pepe isn't your thing, I strongly suggest you make the meatballs and use them with whatever *pastina* you prefer. Guaranteed you're going to love it.

INGREDIENTS

FOR THE MEATBALLS

½ lb ground veal
¼ cup grated cheese, Pecorino Romano
    preferred
½ cup plain bread crumbs
1 large egg, slightly beaten

⅛ tsp nutmeg
zest from ½ lemon
2 TBS fresh parsley, chopped
salt & pepper, to taste

FOR THE SOUP

2 quarts homemade chicken stock - see p 19 - low-sodium store-bought may be
    substituted
1 cup Acini di Pepe, uncooked
additional grated Pecorino Romano

(continued)

DIRECTIONS

TO MAKE THE MEATBALLS

Place all the ingredients into a bowl and mix until combined. Do not overwork.

Use a melon baller or small scoop to fashion small meatballs.

Divide the number of meatballs in half and place each half on separate baking sheets.

Place one baking sheet into the freezer and, once frozen, place the meatballs in a container and return to the freezer for use on a later date.

Use the other half in the soup.

TO PREPARE THE SOUP (MINESTRA)

Bring the stock to a rapid boil.

Add the Acini di Pepe, stir, and then add the remaining half of the meatballs.

When stock returns to the boil, reduce to a medium simmer and cook for about 10 minutes. Stir often but gently so that the meatballs remain intact.

At the end of 10 minutes, taste the minestra to see if the pasta is cooked to your liking and to adjust seasoning, if necessary.

Serve immediately with additional grated Pecorino Romano cheese at the table.

Bartolini: The Next Generation

WHAT'S IN A RISOTTO?

Our risotto had quite a reputation among the branches of my family that did not reside in the two-flat. When our relatives from Cincinnati, at the time the southernmost members of the Clan, came for a visit, they had a standing request that this risotto be served as part of their welcoming dinner. I remember Mom making it for Dad's Mother during her visits with us and risotto was often served when either of the two-flat's families entertained. What made the Bartolini risotto so special? Chicken gizzards, an ingredient that was lacking from almost all other risotto recipes. If you liked gizzards, you loved this risotto. Of course, if you didn't, well, you'd probably go hungry that night. The latter point being responsible for the greatest cover-up in the long and storied history of the Bartolini.

As popular as this dish was with the adults seated at the table, there was one member of the family, my sibling, who would have none of it. The child flat out refused to eat them. Mom, in an effort to get the child to at least eat the rice, told the child that the gizzards were "dried mushrooms" and to put them aside and eat the rice. There's no way so much as a grain of rice would have been eaten if the child knew there were gizzards on that platter. Out of earshot of the child, Mom then turned to me and my other sibling, commanding we keep quiet about this, "Or else!"

Now, there's nothing so unusual about what Mom did. After all, Mothers since the dawn of time have cajoled, bribed, and, yes, even lied to their children, all in the name of good nutrition. (How many broccoli crowns have been hidden in meatloaf throughout the years?) No, the truly surprising thing about this tale is how long the ruse lasted.

We had all gathered at my parents' home for a family dinner, an event that had become more and more rare. The child noticed that Mom was preparing risotto and asked if dried mushrooms were to be included. Hearing that, I started to laugh and, much to Mom's dismay, the cover-up was exposed. The astonishing fact is that the child was now well over 30 years of age! That's right. One "Or else!" from Mom and my sibling and I kept quiet for over 3 decades. Kids today have it easy.

Will the real, dried mushroom hater, please stand up?

(continued)

RISOTTO WITH GIZZARDS

INGREDIENTS

1 TBS butter
1 TBS olive oil
1 lb chicken gizzards & hearts
1 celery stalk
1 carrot
1 medium onion
 2 qts water
2 TBS butter

1 small onion, diced fine
10 button or crimini mushrooms,
    sliced
2 cups Arborio or Carnaroli rice
4 or 5 cups stock - p 19
salt & pepper, to taste
Pecorino Romano cheese - Parmigiano
    may be substituted

DIRECTIONS

Add the butter and olive oil to a saucepan over medium heat. Add the cleaned chicken gizzards and hearts to the pot and sauté for about 10 minutes. The object is to give them a bit of color, not fry them till fully cooked.

Turn the heat to high before adding the onion, celery, carrot, and 2 quarts of water.

Bring to a boil and reduce to a soft simmer. Continue to simmer for 90 minutes, removing and discarding any foam that may rise to the top.

After 90 minutes strain and reserve the stock. Remove the gizzards and hearts and set aside to cool. Remove the vegetables and discard. Combine this stock with the chicken stock in a saucepan and heat but do not allow to boil.

Once cooled to touch, chop the gizzards and hearts to your preference.

In a large sauce pan or deep frying pan, melt the butter over med-high heat. Add the onion and sauté for about 5 minutes. Season with salt and pepper.

Add the mushrooms to the and sauté for a few minutes until some color is achieved.

Add the gizzards and sauté until heated through. The onion should be translucent by this time. Season with salt and pepper.

Add the rice and sauté for another 5 minutes or so to toast it. The grains should be partially opaque.

Reduce the heat to medium, add a ladle or two of hot stock, and stir the rice. Though you needn't stir it constantly, you shouldn't leave it for more than a couple of minutes.

When the stock is all but gone, add another ladle of stock and stir.

Repeat this process again and again until the rice is just about cooked.

This should take about 20 minutes and the risotto should not be gummy but very moist, though not so much as to be a soup.

Taste and add salt & pepper, as needed.

Turn off the heat, add a final ladle of stock, cover the pan, and let the risotto rest for 5 minutes

Add a handful or 2 of grated Pecorino Romano cheese, stir to combine, and place on the serving platter.

Garnish with more grated cheese and serve.

Notes

Add hot stock, not cold or boiling, to the rice while cooking. Cold stock will prolong the cooking process, whereas boiling stock will evaporate when it hits the pan before it can be absorbed by the rice.

When assembling the ingredients needed to prepare risotto, I usually figure on using three cups of stock for every cup of rice to be cooked. I'll add another cup of stock, just to play it safe. I don't want to run out of stock at the very end of cooking process.

BLACK RICE RISOTTO
WITH ROAST DUCK AND PORCINI

INGREDIENTS

5 tbs butter - separated
1 large shallot, chopped fine
1 clove garlic, minced or grated
several oz duck meat leftovers, chopped
1 oz dried porcini mushrooms

1 cup black rice
½ cup dry white wine
about 2 quarts duck stock - p 19
salt and pepper
grated Pecorino Romano cheese,
Parmigiano may be substitute
chopped parsley for garnish

DIRECTIONS

All risotti are prepared in much the same way, Rather than repeat the steps outlined in the previous risotto recipe, I'll just briefly go over the process. Here, the main difference is using duck stock instead of chicken. To make duck stock, follow Mom's Broth recipe - p 19 - using leftovers from a roast duck instead of chicken. To hydrate the mushrooms: soak in very hot water for 30 minutes. Strain the liquid to remove any grit before using.

In a medium sauce pan, melt 3 TBS of butter over med-high heat. Add some finely chopped shallots and sauté until soft. Add the garlic and continue cooking for about a minute before adding the reserved duck meat and the chopped reconstituted porcini mushrooms. Sauté for a few more minutes and then add the rice. Cook the rice, stirring frequently, until the grains are toasted — about 5 minutes. Reduce the heat to medium, add about a half-cup of dry white wine, stir, and cook until almost all the liquid is absorbed. Repeat the process with the heated duck stock, adding more liquid, stirring, and allowing it to be absorbed before adding another ladle or two more. Once the rice is cooked just about to your preference, add another ladle of stock, cover, turn off the heat, and allow to rest for 5 minutes. Next, remove the cover, add 2 TBS of butter and about ½ cup grated Pecorino Romano or Parmigiano Reggiano. Stir well and serve immediately, garnished with more grated cheese.

There are two kinds of Italian black rice, *riso venere*. Both are a medium grain rice, one of which is made by dyeing Arborio rice with squid ink. The other — the one that was used in this recipe — was developed by crossing the storied Asian Forbidden Rice with an Italian variety. This is a whole grain and, much like brown rice, takes a bit longer to cook than, say, Arborio. In fact, it could easily take an hour to prepare black rice risotto. This means that you will need more stock to cook the rice. In the past, I've suggested using a 3 to 1 ratio — meaning 3 parts stock to every part rice — plus an additional cup of stock for good measure. Because of the increased cooking time required for this particular rice, you may need a much as double my original suggestion. Though that may seem excessive, remember that you can always use the leftover stock in any number of ways.

ROAST TURKEY RISOTTO

Perhaps the best parts of the Thanksgiving feast are the leftovers. I love turkey sandwiches and look forward to enjoying them almost as much as I do the dinner. Aside from the sandwiches, I cannot wait to get that turkey carcass into my stock pot. It makes such a delicious broth that I'll enjoy it by the mug as-is, or as the basis of some soup. Of course, I aways set aside 2 quarts of broth so that I can make risotto. The turkey and all of the herbs and spices that were used during the roasting add so much to this dish. It's definitely worth trying.

This turkey risotto is prepared very much like the previous two recipes. The difference being that turkey stock is used instead of chicken or duck. Although I didn't add mushrooms to this risotto, you can easily do so. Add them to the pot when you add the turkey meat and sauté for a few minutes.

INGREDIENTS

6 cups turkey stock - p 19
4 TBS butter - divided
1 small onion, finely chopped
1 clove garlic, minced or grated
7 oz roast turkey, chopped

1¾ cups Arborio or Carnaroli rice
4 oz dry white wine
Pecorino Romano cheese, grated
Parmigiano may be substituted

DIRECTIONS

In a medium sauce pan, melt 2 TBS of butter over med-high heat. Add the finely chopped onion and sauté until soft. Add the garlic, sauté for about a minute, and then add the chopped turkey meat, (This is when you'd add the mushrooms, if using.) Continue to cook for a few minutes. Add the rice and toast it by sautéing it for about 5 minutes, stirring frequently. Lower the heat to medium, add the wine, stir, and cook until almost all has been absorbed. Repeat the process with warmed broth, and stir well. Once absorbed, repeat the process again and again, adding stock and stirring frequently. Typically, it will take about 20 minutes to cook the rice. Taste to be sure. Once the rice is cooked to just about to your preference, add another ladle of stock, cover, turn off the heat, and allow to rest for 5 minutes. Next, remove the cover, add 2 TBS of butter, if desired, and about ½ cup grated Pecorino Romano or Parmigiano Reggiano. Stir well and serve immediately, garnished with more grated cheese.

ZIA MEETS THE POPE

During Mom's illness, there were many evenings during which Zia and I passed the time chatting while watching television. Very often, my travels in Italy were the topic of discussion. I had tried, a number of times, to get Mom to come with me to Italy but her fear of flying was too great. Zia had no such fear. Many of our evening chats ended with, "Well, maybe someday …"

After Mom passed, I continued to go to Michigan to help settle her affairs, as one might expect. During one of those trips, Zia and I decided that we could both use a little vacation and a trip to Italy was planned. The tragedy of 9/11 delayed our holiday and we were to leave for the Old Country the following March. Before leaving, however, I spoke with a friend who was employed by American Express. (This is when AmEx still employed thousands of agents to handle all of your travel needs.) He suggested that we attend the Pope's public Mass, conducted every Wednesday in St. Peter's Square. I agreed and he made the necessary arrangements. Later I called the number he supplied and was told where in Vatican City to fetch our tickets. Being that Zia would be in a wheelchair — the day would be far too long and arduous for her to remain on her feet — the woman said that we would be seated "off to the side with the other disabled." She further explained that after Mass the Holy Father would turn to give us all "a special blessing." I was quite pleased and we were all set to go.

We arrived in Rome on a Thursday. There'd been a transit strike that day and we were lucky to get out of Florence. Over the next few days, we toured the ancient capital. Having been to Rome a few times, I made sure that we didn't miss a church, museum, or marble chunk of the Eternal City. We sipped caffè on the Via Veneto, tossed coins in the Trevi Fountain, got stiff necks in the Sistine Chapel, and never met a gelato we didn't like. We saw — and did — it all. On Tuesday, we travelled to Vatican City, picked up our tickets, and spent the rest of the day sightseeing. After breakfast Wednesday morning, we hailed a taxi and headed back to Vatican City to watch Pope John-Paul II celebrate Mass. By the time we got to St. Peter's, the crowd had already begun to gather. For security purposes, the Square was cordoned off and everyone formed a queue to the right, walking along the colonnade. With me pushing Zia in her wheelchair, we joined them and it really wasn't long before we got to the head of the line where metal detectors waited. A Swiss Guard motioned for us to leave the line and to use a detector reserved for people in our circumstance. Suddenly we were "special," though we'd yet to realize just how much.

Then ...

After passing through the metal detector, we rolled alongside of the throng, passing across the front of the Square. The Altar sat atop a stage directly to our right and the Square, now filling with people, was to our left. When we got to the end of the stage, the Faithful turned to the left to finish circling the Square before being allowed to enter the viewing area from the back. Not us, however. Just before we were to turn, one of the Swiss Guards motioned for us to come to him. We had to cross through the people and once we neared the Guard, he unhooked the velvet rope and indicated that we were to go that way. (See? "Special.") Alone, we made our way down a passageway, wondering all the while what was going on. At its end we had no choice but to turn to the right and now there was a ramp that ran parallel to the passage we had just traversed. Once we started up that ramp, it became clear that we were headed to the stage where the Altar stood.

Dumbfounded, we arrived at the top of the ramp not knowing which way to turn or what to do. Before us was St Peter's Square, filling with people, and to our left was the Altar in the center of a stage that had been divided into large sections, some with seats. A gentleman in a gray tux with tails motioned for us to come to him and he positioned us in a section to the right of where the Altar stood. I was given a chair and sat next to Zia in her wheelchair. The Pope would say Mass directly in front of us. Across, on the other side of the Altar, some newlywed couples sat dressed in their wedding finery. To their side were children, some of whom had apparently recently received their First Holy Communion. The view from that side was partly blocked by sound and lighting equipment. For reasons that would soon become clear, our view had no such obstructions. No one, save the

(continued)

Cardinals that attended him, would have a better view of that Mass than did Zia on that day. Needless to say, I was in a state of utter disbelief and Zia, wiping away tears, thanked me profusely. But wait, there's more.

After what seemed like an eternity, we could hear a roar rising from the crowd. At the other end of the Square, the Pope could be seen riding the pope mobile through the faithful. A few minutes later, he was riding up a ramp, passing between us and the Altar, naught but a few feet separating us. Had we left Vatican City right then, Zia would have been one very happy Bartolini — but there's still more to this tale.

The Pope said Mass a mere 20 feet before us and the service took a little longer than one might expect since he delivered his sermon in three languages: Italian, English, and Polish. All the while Zia tearfully thanked me. It was near the end of the Mass when things really got interesting. I was standing for the final prayers when another man dressed in a gray tuxedo with tails indicated that he wanted me. He was standing behind the altar, out-of-sight of the congregation, and as I stepped forward, all I could think was that this cannot be good. As I've said many times since, if I could have found a way to hide, to 'blend in", I surely would have. But when you're one of the few standing on a stage in an area meant for wheel chairs, you're a tad bit conspicuous. With no place to hide, I stepped forward and he immediately made it clear that he wanted me to push Zia. So, I pushed my bewildered Zia the 20 or so feet towards him and, as I did, others in wheelchairs began to queue up behind us. When we got to him, he turned her chair so that we were facing the crowd. We then realized what was in store. About 15 feet before us was another similarly attired gentleman who began to wave us on. Our gentleman gave me a shove and suddenly we were leading a procession to meet Pope John-Paul II. Poor Zia. By the time we reached the "waving man", the two of us were a mess. Zia was sobbing and I frantically searched the clouded sky fully expecting my death by lightning bolt. We turned to the left and there, 5 feet before us, stood His Holiness who, at this point in his life, was quite frail. Dressed in his familiar white robes, he stood, hunched over facing away from us. We approached and, as if Cecil B. DeMille was in control of the lighting, the sun burst through the clouds. as Pope John Paul turned to face us. We were both struck by how blue his eyes were, especially when contrasted against his pale complexion and now gleaming white vestments. Stunning does not begin to describe the effect. Shock turned to awe as he smiled, grabbed Zia's hand, and blessed us. Within seconds, we were on our way towards another waving man who directed us to an "exit ramp." Soon we were heading back to the Square. Along the way, we decided that we'd leave immediately.

We reached the bottom of the ramp and through the corridor we rushed. When we re-entered the Square, there, on the 2 Jumbotrons for all to see, was a photo of our meeting the Holy Father, Zia in tears and me looking like a deer in headlights. No, we do not have that picture. We were asked if we wanted a picture taken when we were first situated on the stage but we misunderstood, thinking he was going to take a picture of us seated there. Remember, we didn't know that we were going to actually meet the Pope. With our ginormous faces looming above, I quickly pushed Zia through St. Peter's Square and out on to the street. Virtually no one else had left yet but then again few, if any, had received the full Papal treatment that we had already experienced. So, with little competition, we easily hailed a cab and within minutes were on our way back to our hotel, all the while Zia continued to wipe away tears as she thanked me.

Now

Once there, we skipped lunch, preferring to retire to our rooms. We had anticipated a memorable day and this was so much more than that, a truly once-in-a-lifetime experience. A rest was definitely in order. Later that afternoon, as was our custom, room service delivered our caffè to Zia's room. Normally, we would have planned our dinner and evening but, that night, we decided to "stay close to home" and made an early reservation at a restaurant just down the street from where we were staying.

Not that much later, we were seated at the restaurant, our appetites still nowhere to be found. Now, one thing you should know about my Cara Zia is that she loves pasta every bit as much as I do. When we dined, we always enjoyed a primo piatto of pasta of some sort before ordering our secondi and contorni. So, absent an appetite, we did what came naturally: we ordered pasta. That dish happened to be Spaghetti alla Carbonara which, not so coincidentally, just happens to be the next recipe to be shared.

SPAGHETTI ALLA CARBONARA

Mom first prepared this dish for me when I was in my teens. She told me a legend: its name was derived from the coal miners who worked in the mines that were near Rome. As they ate their lunch, which often consisted of a plate of pasta, coal dust fell from their clothes and on to their plates. The dish's ample use of black pepper is an homage, of sorts, to those miners and their lunches.

The version Mom served me usually contained bacon although prosciutto was sometimes substituted, albeit rarely. Pancetta just wasn't something that Mom and Zia used in their cooking. To be truly authentic, seek *guanciale*, a cured pork product made from a pig's jowls and which, like this dish, originated in the region of Lazio.

INGREDIENTS

1 TBS salt
1 lb spaghetti
3 eggs, beaten
1 cup grated Pecorino Romano cheese – separated
2 TBS extra virgin olive oil
4 oz. guanciale, ¼ inch dice - pancetta, prosciutto, bacon, or ham may be substituted
1 or 2 cloves of garlic, sliced
½ to 1 tsp freshly cracked black pepper
reserved pasta water
Pecorino or Parmigiano cheese for garnish/serving

DIRECTIONS

Warm a large pasta serving bowl in a 200° F oven or by pouring hot water over it.

Bring a 6 to 8 quart pot of water to boil. Add the salt & spaghetti and stir.

Check the spaghetti package's cooking instructions. You'll want it to be 2 minutes shy of al dente when the rest of the ingredients are ready.

To a large mixing bowl, add half of the cheese to the 3 eggs and beat well to be rid of any lumps.

In a large, deep frying pan, heat the oil over medium heat. Add the pancetta and brown, rendering all the fat. Do not over cook.

Add the garlic and sauté for about a minute.

While the garlic cooks, reserve a cup of pasta water, drain the pasta, and add the pasta to the frying pan.

Continue cooking the pasta in the oil mixture for 2 minutes, heating it thoroughly.

Pour the frying pan's contents into the warmed serving bowl.

Add the egg and cheese mixture to the bowl in a slow, steady stream, stirring constantly to prevent the eggs from scrambling. Once fully coated, add the remaining cheese, the pepper, and as much pasta water as necessary to create a creamy sauce.

Serve immediately with plenty of grated cheese and cracked black pepper available at the table.

Note: To avoid scrambling the eggs, temper them by adding a bit of the hot pasta water into the egg-cheese mixture before pouring it all into the hot pasta.

MAIN COURSES
SECONDI PIATTI

Zia Lea and Uncle Al shortly after becoming engaged

Dad and the Catch of the Day: Coho Salmon

FOR THE LOVE OF COD

Wind drying and salting are among the oldest methods of preserving food known to Man. For hundreds of years, both methods have been used to preserve cod. In Italy, cod that has been both wind-dried and salted is called *baccalà*, whereas cod that has been only wind-dried is known as *stoccafisso*. No matter which method was used to preserve the fish, it must be well-rinsed before cooking. This is easily accomplished by placing it in a large baking dish filled with cold water and changing the water occasionally over the course of the next 2 days. I find it helps to let the water run gently into the dish a few times, as well. You will know when the fish is ready by its appearance, feel, and, yes, its smell. Be careful, however, not to run the water too forcefully. The fish could lose its firm texture and might even disintegrate.

Now about that smell ...

Both baccalà and stoccafisso have a distinct odor that "comes to life" when it is first rinsed. Stoccafisso, however, is by far the worst. In the warm months Grandpa would soak his stoccafisso outside in the backyard, all the while hoping that our dogs would be enough to keep the cats away. Winter, however, posed a problem.

I was about 5 or 6 years old and shared a bedroom with my brother, Paul, who was about 10 or 11 years old at the time. Our bedroom, as well as the bedroom of my cousins' directly above ours, was separated from the rest of the house by a stairwell that ran from the 2nd floor to the basement. One morning Mom entered our bedroom in a cleaning frenzy, convinced that my brother or I had done, or left, something disgusting in the room. A foul stench had reached her kitchen which was located on the other side of the stairwell. Angels that we were and despite our claims of godliness, our bedroom was declared Ground Zero. Lucky for us, Mom found nothing untoward in our room and now, more determined than ever, she set out to find the source of the stench. It wasn't long before her nose led her to the basement where, under the stairs, she found Grandpa's stoccafisso, bathing innocently in a tub of water. Revenge is a dish best served cold, so, Mom patiently bided her time. When Grandpa left later that morning for his daily rounds, she placed the tub of stoccafisso under his bed and closed his bedroom door as she left. Even Grandpa's Old Spice, the scent of which permeated that room, proved to be no match for stoccafisso, as Grandpa learned when he opened that door a few hours later. To be sure, Mom and her Father "discussed" the matter but I was too young to be privy to that "chat". Mom must have driven a hard bargain, though, for Grandpa never did soak stoccafisso under those stairs again.

BACCALÀ ALLA MARCHIGIANA

Regardless of the reason, baccalà wasn't cooked in our home but, lucky for me both Zia and Nonna were masters of its preparation. As a result, as Zia Lea recalls, I was forever trying to snag whatever leftovers I could from their meal. Although both women used the same ingredients, Nonna preferred to bake her baccalà, while Zia cooked hers atop the stove. As one who "sampled" both preparations, I can attest that each method produced a delicious dish. As you'll soon see, Zia and I combined both methods, partially cooking the dish atop the stove before finishing it off in the oven.

INGREDIENTS

3 to 4 medium-sized potatoes, peeled
    and quartered
olive oil
salt & pepper, to taste
3 TBS olive oil
1 medium onion, chopped
2 cloves garlic, minced

3 TBS fresh parsley, chopped
2 tsp marjoram
1 large can (28 oz) tomatoes - whole or
    diced
1 lb baccalà, soaked - p 129 - and cut
    into 3 inch pieces
salt and pepper to taste

DIRECTIONS

Pre-heat oven to 400° F.

Season potatoes with salt and pepper, toss with a splash of olive oil, and roast on a baking sheet for 20 minutes at 400° F.

Meanwhile, in a large, oven-proof frying pan, heat olive oil over med-high heat. Add the onion and sauté until translucent, about 5 minutes

Add garlic and parsley and continue to sauté for another minute.

Add tomatoes & marjoram, bring to boil, reduce to simmer, and cook uncovered for 30 minutes. If sauce is "tight", add water.

Add roasted potatoes and continue simmering for another 20 minutes. Add water if necessary.

Add baccalà to the tomato sauce and place pan into the 400° F oven. Bake for 20 minutes. Taste before seasoning with salt & pepper, if necessary.

Serve immediately.

GRILLED BACCALÀ

The family breading mixture seems meant for seafood, in general, and baccalà, in particular. Although wonderful grilled, this recipe can also be baked in the oven. Just prepare it as you would for the grill but place the fillet(s) on a lightly oiled baking dish/sheet and bake on the center rack of a pre-heated 375° F oven for about 15 minutes. The fish will be moist and flake easily when done.

INGREDIENTS

1 lb baccalà, soaked - p 129
breading mixture - p 22
fresh lemon juice

DIRECTIONS

Pat dry freshly rinsed baccalà fillet(s) using a paper towel.

Coat both sides of the fillets with the breading and carefully place in a grilling basket. Securely close it to prevent the fish falling apart at the end of the cooking process.

Pre-heat the grill.

Once secured, lay the basket on the grill and sprinkle a bit of olive oil over the fillet's top side and close the grill's lid. Lower the heat to med-high.

Depending upon your grill's temperature, how the basket rests on the grill plates, and the thickness of the fillet(s), baccalà will take from 8 to 11 minutes per side to cook. Be sure to check it midway through the cooking of each side and be prepared to adjust cooking times, as required.

Once you've flipped the basket over, sprinkle the fish's new top side with the juice of a half-lemon. Continue grilling until done.

Carefully remove from the grilling basket and serve immediately.

Notes:
When grilling any fish, you will greatly improve your odds for success by cleaning the grilling surface very well and oiling it before placing the fish on it.

If you cannot find salted cod, fresh cod, haddock, or pollack can be substituted.

BAKED WHITING
MERLUZZO

This recipe goes back at least 50 years. I cannot say how long it had been since I last saw merluzzo and was quite surprised to see it one morning at the market. I couldn't wait to get some home and call Zia for the recipe. As it turned out, this is pretty much the same method we Bartolini use when preparing most fish. Our breading is perfectly suited for seafood, adding a great deal of flavor to the dish while keeping the seafood moist during the cooking process.

INGREDIENTS

whole whiting, cleaned and scaled
⅓ cup breading mixture per fish - p 22
fresh lemon juice
salt and pepper

DIRECTIONS

Season each fish, inside and out, with salt and pepper,

If you wish, squeeze a bit of lemon juice into the breading.

Stuff the body cavity with the breading mixture.

Place the fish on a lightly oiled baking sheet. Sprinkle the remaining breading on top of the fish.

Bake in a pre-heated 375° F oven for 20 minutes are until the breading is golden brown.

Serve immediately.

Note: When I first shared our recipe, there was some discussion over what fish is actually merluzzo. My Italian fishmonger assured me that here in the U.S., whiting is known as merluzzo. Friends on the other side of the Atlantic stated that there, merluzzo is actually hake. From what I've learned, both fish are members of the cod family and distant cousins.

STOVETOP BRAISED RABBIT

Rabbit is easy to prepare and even easier to ruin. Its meat is surprisingly lean and, as a result, not very tender. This means that it can be both dry and tough if not cooked properly. A slow, long braise is a good way to get around the problem. The recipe presented here is our family's traditional method of cooking rabbit.

When I first started cooking rabbit, it was disastrous -- ask my Traveling Companion, Jaime. I just couldn't get the braising right. After a few attempts, I tried cooking it like Mom cooked *chicken cacciatore* -- p 156. If you have problems with the braise I've outlined, try to cook it *alla cacciatore*. You will not be disappointed.

INGREDIENTS

1 dressed rabbit, about 3 lbs.
olive oil
2 cloves garlic, chopped
1 tomato, chopped - 2 TBS tomato paste
      may be substituted

2 sprigs of fresh rosemary
white wine
salt and pepper

DIRECTIONS

Cut the rabbit into manageable pieces. This can be from 8 to 12 pieces, depending upon your preference and plans for serving.

Season the rabbit with salt and pepper.

Heat a few TBS of olive oil over med-high heat in a deep frypan with a lid.

Place the garlic and rabbit pieces into the pan and brown the rabbit before flipping them over to brown the other side --- about 5 or 6 minutes per side.

Add the tomato, rosemary, and about ¾ cups of white wine, to start, and bring the pan to the boil.

Reduce the heat to a soft simmer, cover, and braise the rabbit for no less than an hour -- more like an hour-and-a-half.

During the braise, turn the pieces over occasionally and add more wine, as needed, should the pan begin to dry.

When fully cooked, taste to see if salt or pepper is needed. Remove and discard the rosemary sprigs, place the rabbit on a platter, and serve.

GRANDPA'S BARBECUE

The two-flat had a great barbecue in the backyard that Grandpa built during the summer of 1959. Grandpa was a master at masonry and he created the arch over the grilling area without any means of support. (It wasn't until I was much older that I appreciated the skill involved in doing that.) The grilling area had 3 sections: the top was the grill surface; the middle was where the fire burned; and the lowest section was where the ashes collected. The doors of the lower 2 sections had vents with which you could limit and direct the airflow to the fire, and thereby control the grill's heat. The flue system practically guaranteed that there would be no smoke to bother the eyes of the barbecue's many users. To the left of the grilling area was a large, flat surface that served as a work station and, under that, an area for storing wood. He'd thought of everything.

Once it was finished, that barbecue was often the center of activity for both households regardless of the weather. In winter, our yard was turned into an ice skating rink and the grill helped to warm us as it heated our hot chocolate. In warmer weather I clearly remember seeing Dad, the High Priest of Grilling, standing in front of his altar, umbrella in his left hand, struggling with the wind and rain, as his right hand tended to the sacrificed beast that would become our meal. Once summer came, there were many Sundays when both families feasted together on the patio. While the men gathered at the barbecue, the women ferried supplies to the dinner table -- no small feat when feeding 12+ people.

Hindsight being what it is, Grandpa was wise to build that barbecue first, before all else. Without it, I doubt the two families would have shared so many dinners together. Without those meals, life in the two-flat would have been, well, boring.

GRANDPA'S GRILLED SHRIMP

Where the barbecue was often a center of activity for both households, there were plenty of times when one could find Grandpa out back grilling something for his lunch. This was particularly true on Fridays, when he'd be grilling seafood, often shrimp. Somehow, I always found myself at his side as he grilled and, lo and behold, he would give me 1 or 2 shrimp just for "keeping company." I think I got the better part of that deal. Not only did I get a couple of shrimp but now, years later, whenever I lay skewers of shrimp on a grill, my thoughts inevitably turn to the times spent standing next to my Grandpa in front of his master work — and I smile.

INGREDIENTS

1 lb large shrimp (no smaller than
    21 – 25 ct), de-veined but not
    peeled

about ½ cup breading mixture - p 22
salt & pepper, to taste
lemon wedges for serving

DIRECTIONS

Soak wooden skewers for at least one hour before use.

Place the shrimp and the breading mixture into a bowl, mix, season with salt and pepper, cover, and refrigerate for at least 30 minutes. Pre-heat the grill.

Use 2 skewers to hold the shrimp. Depending upon the size of the shrimp, you may be able to skewer from 3 to 6 shrimp per pair of skewers. Place a bit of the stuffing between the shrimp.

Place the shrimp on the hot grill plates or in a grill basket. It may take 2 minutes per side, or, a few more depending upon the heat of the fire.

Leaving the shells on the shrimp will protect them from burning, Even so, do not leave the grill while the shrimp are cooking.

Serve the shrimp as-is on the skewers or off of the skewers and arranged on a platter with plenty of lemon wedges.

MOM'S CITY CHICKEN

We all loved these skewers and Mom served them often on Summer evenings
when Dad was home for dinner. He grilled them and I can almost smell the aromas
of burning charcoal and bacon as he worked. Today, these bite-sized pieces of
skewered meat make great finger food for a backyard party or barbecue.

INGREDIENTS

Pork, cut into 1½ inch cubes
Veal, cut into 1½ inch cubes
Beef, cut into 1½ inch cubes
Bacon, 1 slice for every skewer

marinade - p 23
juice and zest of 1 lemon

DIRECTIONS

Soak wooden skewers in water for at least an hour before use.

Add the lemon juice and zest to the bowl containing the marinade. Stir to combine and reserve a ¼ cup for later use.

Place the meats into the bowl with the marinade mixture, toss until coated, and refrigerate for at least one hour or overnight.

When ready, light the grill.

Using one thick skewer or 2 thin for each city chicken, pierce one end of a bacon rasher, followed by one piece of each type of meat. Be sure that the top piece of meat for each skewer is pork. After the pork is in place, wrap the meats with the bacon and secure its remaining end by piercing it with the skewer(s) tip(s).

Once finished and the grill is hot, shut down part of the grill to facilitate indirect grilling. Use a rag dipped in oil to grease the grill plate.

Place the skewered meat on the the grill over the section where the flames have been turned off with the pork closest to the fire/heat. This is why you place the pork on the top of each skewer.

Turn the meat after a few minutes, more or less depending upon the grill's heat. The object is to cook the skewered meat without torching the bacon.

The pork, being closest to the fire, will cook faster.

With the meat still very rare, move the skewers directly over the fire/heat.

Now the object is to crisp the bacon and to finish cooking the skewered meats. Turn the skewers occasionally to ensure even cooking.

When grilled to your satisfaction, remove to a platter, brush with reserved marinade, and serve.

GRILLED RACK OF SPRING LAMB

Rack of Spring Lamb is a fantastic cut of meat, perfect for any celebratory meal. Yes, it can be expensive but you may be able to find partial racks for sale on Easter Sunday or the day after. Butchers, having trimmed larger racks for special orders, are eager to sell these smaller portions.

INGREDIENTS

rack of spring lamb, 7 or 8 ribs,
french cut
2 cloves garlic, minced
1 TBS fresh rosemary, chopped

1 cup marinade - p 23
salt and pepper, to taste
fresh parsley, chopped, for garnish

DIRECTIONS

A couple of hours before you are to grill the lamb, remove it from the refrigerator and place on a pie plate or similar dish.

Season with garlic, rosemary, salt, and pepper before sprinkling the marinade.

Set aside to marinate until you're ready to cook. If your kitchen is warm, place the marinating rack in the fridge until 30 minutes before you intend to cook it.

Pre-heat your barbecue on high. Wrap the chop tips with aluminum foil.

Place the rack directly over the heat and sear the meat for a couple of minutes before moving it to an area on the grill away from the heat.

Use an instant read thermometer. The meat is cooked when it reaches a temperature of about 120° F for rare.

Allow to rest, covered, for 5 minutes before serving garnished with a bit of parsley (optional).

SNAILS
LUMACHE

Because of the cleaning involved, lumache were rarely served at the two-flat. Now available in cans, back then they had to be soaked to rouse them from dormancy, scrubbed, boiled, scrubbed again, and either removed from their shells or left intact for further cooking. Mom put water, vinegar, and the dormant lumache into her largest pot; placed a colander atop the pot, weighted with a heavy book or pan; and, set it aside to let the lumache come out of their shells. As they came to life, they would head up into the colander, the heavy weight keeping both snails and colander in place. Fortunately, that weight wasn't heavy enough to prevent me from snatching a pet when I was about 6 years old. It was, however, too heavy for me to replace properly before I returned to bed, my new pet snail in a water glass at my bedside. Imagine Mom's delight when she awoke to find snails crawling all over her kitchen walls and my new pet heading for my bedroom ceiling. It should come as no surprise that I never had another pet snail.

INGREDIENTS

2 TBS extra virgin olive oil
1 large onion, chopped
3 garlic cloves, diced
1 can (14 oz) diced tomatoes
1 can (14 oz) crushed tomatoes

4 oz dry white wine
3 TBS parsley
1 tsp marjoram
1 can (15 oz, 48 count) very large
size lumache
salt & pepper, to taste

DIRECTIONS

Heat olive oil in medium-sized sauce pan over med-high heat.

Add onions and sauté until translucent, about 5 minutes. Season lightly with salt & pepper.

Add garlic and sauté for another minute before adding the tomatoes, wine, marjoram, and parsley.

Bring to a boil, reduce to a simmer, and continue cooking for about 45 minutes or until the tomatoes are cooked and the sauce has darkened.

Add the lumache with the canning liquid and continue to simmer for about 30 minutes more. The sauce should be dark and thick.

Season with salt & pepper to taste and serve as-is in a bowl or use it to dress your favorite pasta.

MOM'S BRAISED LAMB SHANKS

I guess I've inherited Mom's love of lamb shanks and, thankfully, her recipe, as well. Over the years, I have made a few changes, the biggest being that I now braise the shanks in a slow cooker. If, like Mom, you prefer to braise yours in the oven, I've added those instructions at the end of the recipe. Any other changes I've made are noted in the recipe. Whether you choose to follow my changes, you're in for a very special dish.

INGREDIENTS

2 tbsp olive oil
6 cloves of garlic, smashed, separated
2 lamb shanks trimmed of excess fat
2 medium carrots, roughly chopped
1 cup leaves and stalks from the top of
    a celery heart, chopped
1 onion, sliced
2 tbsp tomato paste

4 sprigs of rosemary
1 bay leaf
¾ cup sherry vinegar - optional (Mom
    didn't use any vinegar)
1 cup white wine (Mom used red wine)
vegetable stock (Mom used chicken)
salt & pepper to taste
lemon zest for garnish, optional

DIRECTIONS

In a large fry pan, heat the olive oil over med-high heat.

Add 2 smashed garlic cloves and sauté until golden. Remove the garlic and discard.

Season the lamb shanks with salt and pepper and place them into the pan, browning them on all sides. This could take anywhere from 10 to 15 minutes.

Remove and reserve the lamb shanks.

Place all the vegetables into the pan, season with salt and pepper, and sauté until some color is achieved.

Add the tomato paste and cook until fragrant and its color deepens, 2 to 3 minutes.

Remove the mixture from the pan and place into the slow cooker, along with the remaining garlic, rosemary, bay leaf, and sherry vinegar.

Use the white wine to deglaze the pan and then add it to the slow cooker. Season with salt & pepper.

Place the lamb shanks into the pot and add enough vegetable stock so that half of the shanks are submerged. Do NOT completely cover with stock. Cover the slow cooker.

Cook on low for 8 hours, turning over the shanks once during the cooking process

Remove meat and cover. Strain the liquids, place in a sauce pan, and reduce to half.

Sauce may then be served as-is or can be thickened using some flour, corn starch, or arrowroot.

Serve, garnished with lemon zest (optional) and with the sauce on the side.

Note: To cook shanks in the oven

Preheat the oven to 350° F.

Increase the amount of liquids: use 1 cup dry white wine, the same amount of vinegar, and enough stock until shanks are ⅔ submerged. Do NOT completely cover with liquid.

Cook for about 2 hours. Meat should be fork tender and just about falling off the bone. Let it go too long and it will fall of the bone, ruining your presentation.

ROAST GOAT

Up until I was about 5 years of age, a baby goat was the Bartolini roast of choice for celebrations. As Zia Lea recalls, a young goat was prepared for each of the 6 of our births — my 2 siblings and 3 cousins. I recall goat being served for Easter when I was very young. Against Mom's orders, I went down into the basement one year and found the kid. I barely had time to say, "Awww!" before I felt a tap on my shoulder and a well-placed hand on my behind as I was ushered back up the stairs. Even so, of the 2 of us kids in the basement that evening, I fared far better than the four-legged one. That night, long after we kids of the two-legged variety were in bed, Dad went into the basement and "prepared" the goat for the holiday meal. As I recall, that was the last year that roast goat was served. Lamb replaced it as the meat of choice for Easter. That didn't last long, however, because my siblings weren't at all fond of lamb. Mom switched to some other roast, I'm sure, but, as I've mentioned before, my attention was focused upon the platter of ravioli. Nothing else on that table mattered.

INGREDIENTS

olive oil
1 goat shoulder roast, about 4 lbs
4 whole garlic cloves
rosemary
salt and pepper
1 cup dry white wine
the juice of ½ lemon

about a dozen new potatoes or 3 large
cut into equal-sized pieces
all-purpose flour
stock (chicken or vegetable)
dry white wine
butter
lemon zest for garnish

DIRECTIONS

Pre-heat oven to 350° F.

Place a couple TBS olive oil in a roasting pan with lid over med-high heat.

Add the goat and brown on all sides.

Place the garlic, rosemary stems, lemon juice, and wine into the pan, cover, and place all into the pre-heated oven.

After 15 minutes, add the potatoes to the pan, stir, cover, and return to the oven.

After 45 minutes more, remove the pan's lid, again stir the potatoes, raise the oven temperature to 375° F, and roast — lid off — for another 15 minutes.

Goat will be ready when it reaches a temperature of 145° F. Let rest covered for 15 minutes before serving.

While the roast rests, add an amount of flour equal to the amount of juices in the pan's bottom. Over medium heat, stir them to make a roux and allow to cook for a couple of minutes. Add a little stock, and then wine, to make a sauce, stirring constantly to prevent lumps while the sauce thickens. Add as much wine and/or stock needed to get the consistency that you wish. Check for seasoning, take it off the heat, and add a tbsp of butter to finish the sauce before serving.

Serve the goat with the sauce, garnished with fresh lemon zest, if desired.

NONNA KNOWS BEST

Tripe, *trippa*, is a type of offal made from the stomach of usually beef or sheep. It was not a dish enjoyed by everyone at the two-flat, nor was polenta. In fact, Mom hated the latter because it reminded her of her childhood during the Great Depression. (She finally started eating it again many years later.) Grandpa, however, loved trippa and often asked Stefanina -- Uncle's mother and whom we all called "Nonna" -- to make trippa for him. Very often, it was served atop polenta.

On those occasions, the aroma of some as yet unknown delicacy, wafting down the stairs was my siren call. A quick run up the back stairs and a stealth bomber-like cruise through their kitchen was all I needed to check things out. Trippa was on the menu! I returned home via the front stairs and then the wait began in my room. After what seemed like an eternity, I would hear Nonna's voice calling, "Johnny! Johnny, are you there? I've got surprise for you." My feet couldn't get me up those stairs

JUL 60
Nonna with Lucky

fast enough. When I burst into the kitchen, she'd be standing there, smiling broadly, holding a dinner plate. "Would you like some polenta?" Trying not to appear too eager, I'd reply with something like, "Sure." And so the lesson began. "This is how you make polenta, Johnny." Holding the plate in one hand, she would use the other hand's fingers to dot the plate's surface with dabs of butter. Then she would sprinkle the plate with freshly ground Pecorino Romano cheese.

Next using a large spoon, Nonna would slowly and carefully cover the plate with a nice layer of freshly made polenta By now, I was about to drool. "Pazienza, Johnny," and she would dot the surface of the polenta with more butter, to be followed with another sprinkle of grated cheese. Then came the trippa. Da Vinci didn't take such care painting the Mona Lisa as did this dear woman when she layered the trippa upon that polenta. Then came another sprinkle of cheese. Every time when she was done, with a twinkle in her eye, she would hand me the plate and say, "This is how you make polenta with trippa."

Many years later, I prepared trippa with polenta for Mom and Zia Lea. They were dumbstruck when I prepared their plates just as Nonna had once showed me. Although both were aware that she often fixed me a plate, neither had any idea how that plate was crafted. Today, some 40+ years after my last serving of Nonna's cooking, I cannot prepare a dish of polenta with trippa without hearing her say, "Pazienza." When my plate is ready, I just have to echo, "This is how you make polenta with trippa."

NONNA'S TRIPPA

INGREDIENTS

5 lbs honeycomb tripe
3 TBS extra virgin olive oil
¼ lb pancetta, chopped
1 large onion, chopped
4 TBS fresh parsley, chopped, separated
4 garlic cloves, diced
½ cup dry white wine
3 TBS tomato paste

1 large can (28 oz) crushed tomatoes
1 large can (28 oz) diced tomatoes
1 small onion, whole, studded with 5 or 6 whole cloves
1 TBS marjoram
salt & pepper, to taste
grated Pecorino Romano cheese

DIRECTIONS

Trim trippa, discarding unusable parts. Place in a large pot, cover with water, and bring to a boil. Reduce heat and simmer uncovered for 1 hour.

Remove trippa from water. When cool enough to handle, cut into strips 1 to 2 inches in length and about ⅓ inch wide.

While the trippa cools, heat olive oil in a medium-sized sauce pan over med-high heat. Add pancetta and sauté until cooked but not crisp, about 8 minutes.

Add the chopped onion, half of the parsley, and sauté until the onion is translucent, about 5 minutes. Season with salt & pepper to taste.

Add garlic and sauté for another minute before adding the wine. Cook until the wine is reduced and almost gone.

Add the tomato paste and continue to sauté for 2 minutes before adding the tomatoes, marjoram, and trippa. Season with salt & pepper, stir well, and then add the clove-studded onion.

Bring to a boil, reduce to a simmer, and cook for at least 2 hours. Sauce should be dark and thick; the trippa tender.

Remove studded onion and discard. Add most of the remaining parsley to the pot, taste to see if additional salt or pepper is needed, and stir well.

Serve immediately -- over polenta? -- garnished with the remaining parsley. and a sprinkling of cheese.

ZIA'S BAKED CALAMARI

Zia Lea's stuffed calamari have reached legendary status with my generation of the Bartolini Clan. It's a very special night when she serves them for dinner. Photos of the serving platter are sure to be sent to those not present at the table. Give this recipe a try and you'll find out why.

INGREDIENTS

3 lbs calamari with tentacles
2 cups Bartolini breading mixture - p 22
1 TBS lemon juice

DIRECTIONS

Check to make sure the squid are all clean. Remove the beak from the center of each set of tentacles, if present.

If using, chop the tentacles and add to the breading mixture. Add the lemon juice and mix well.

Preheat oven to 350° F.

Use the breading to stuff each squid tube. Do not pack nor overstuff. The calamari will shrink while baking.

Place the stuffed calamari in a single layer into a lightly greased baking dish/pan/sheet.

When all are stuffed, place the baking dish into the pre-heated oven. Bake for 30 to 35 minutes.

Remove from oven and serve immediately.

Note: In the unlikely event that you have leftovers, coarsely chop them and add them to pan of Aglio e Olio - p 96 - just as you combine the rest of the ingredients. Give it a good toss and serve. *Fantastico!*

THIS QUAIL IS NO PIGEON

INGREDIENTS

cooked pasta
3 TBS olive oil
1 small to medium onion, chopped
3 TBS parsley, chopped
3 cloves garlic, diced
4 whole quail, dressed

1 large can (28 oz) tomatoes
½ tsp marjoram
4 oz white wine
salt & pepper
Pecorino Romano cheese, grated

DIRECTIONS

Heat oil in a large, heavy-bottomed pot over med-high heat.

Add onion and sauté for about 5 minutes before adding garlic and parsley.

Continue to sauté until fragrant, about a minute.

Add quail to the pot and LIGHTLY brown on all sides.

Remove quail and add remaining ingredients to the pot. Mix well and bring to the boil.

Return quail to the pot and return to the boil before reducing the heat to a soft simmer. Cook until done, about 30 to 45 minutes.

Remove quail to a serving dish.

Use sauce to dress the pasta, reserving some for use at the table.

Garnish the pasta with grated cheese and place both pasta and quail on a large serving platter.

Zia and I prepared this dish during a recent visit home. I had intended to bring pigeons so that I could record how they were prepared back in the day. The only problem was that I couldn't source them except for one place not far from my home. Unfortunately, I was there once when an order for pigeons was placed and witnessed their "preparation". Their handling was beyond rough and I could never purchase a pigeon there. Now, I'm fully aware of how meat comes to be displayed in our markets and, over the years, have watched more than my fair share of poultry "prepared" for our dinners. Hard as it may be for some to believe, there are comparatively humane ways to do this. When I see evidence to the contrary, I find another place to shop and something else to eat. So, with quail more readily available, we substituted it for the pigeon in today's recipe. Besides, I think you'll find the next story a bit more enjoyable if we cook quail here.

Note: Regardless whether you cook quail or pigeon, there is one rule you must follow: do not over-brown the bird. Both are small and their meat, being relatively lean, will dry out very quickly when overcooked. Keep an eye on the birds when you place them into the hot pan and you'll do fine.

DUKE, DUKE, DUKE, DUKE'S A GIRL!

Although pigeon was prepared for dinner at the old two-flat, it certainly wasn't served frequently or with any regularity. It was simply a matter of supply, for it wasn't every day that you could find enough pigeons to prepare and serve. The family did have its sources though. One, a workmate of Uncle Al, bred pigeons and often gave us young birds that didn't meet his standards. Of course, there was the farmers market and I often watched as Grandpa haggled with the vendor over an amount as little as a quarter. In reality, this was all a game and I had a front row seat. It's not like there were dozens of vendors selling young pigeons. Nor were there throngs of people queuing at their stalls demanding the birds. Grandpa and the vendor haggled a bit but both knew all along that the deal had been struck the

"Legs" Bartolini with Duke and Skipper, my first dog

moment Grandpa walked up to the vendor's stall. For me, it was part of the fun of going with Grandpa to the market. The third source for pigeon was from Grandpa's farmer friend. Yes, this was the same Cook's farm where our dogs went, never to be seen again. I must have been about 6 or 7 years old when Grandpa brought home one very young pigeon. Today, the source of this bird is a point of debate.

There are those who think it came from Uncle Al's friend while others believe it came from the farmer. No matter its origin, this bird, being a loner, wasn't destined for the table. "Duke" would become one of the most memorable pets that ever shared the two-flat with us.

Though it may sound odd to have a pigeon as a pet, Duke was only one of many animals that found their way to our home. There were dogs, fish, rabbits, turtles, chameleons, frogs, birds, Chinese pheasants, and even a snake, though the snake's stay was quite brief before being set free in the yard. Our neighbor, Mrs. A, wasn't happy about that. For years, whenever she spotted a snake in her garden, it was ours that she saw. It was just our luck to have found and let loose the Methuselah of snakes. Poor, long-suffering Mrs. A. She was a wonderful woman who treated us kids very kindly. This despite our snake taking up residence in her garden, and, Duke roosting outside her bedroom window every night. That window ledge would never be the same.

Now, Duke was no ordinary pigeon nor pet, for that matter. First of all, Duke was actually a Duchess — having laid an egg under Zia's sofa. It didn't seem to mind having a masculine name so Duke she remained. She was ever-present. If you were in the backyard, Duke was sure to appear, swooping down from above. If you were eating a snack somewhere outside, Duke would find you quicker than the dog and wait for a piece of whatever it was you were eating. Even so, she was most closely attached to Grandpa and Nonna.

When we first moved into the parish and until the early 1960s, the church and school were in the same building. There were a number of masses held every Sunday,. The 9:00 am mass was for us kids. Every Sunday morning at 10:00 AM, Nonna and Grandpa would walk down the street to the church with Duke circling overhead. When it was warm, Duke would wait for them from her perch atop the building or in a nearby tree. On cold or wet days, she'd take refuge in one of the sconces that flanked each entrance to the building, its damaged pane allowing the bird access. Once mass was finished, Duke waited for Nonna and Grandpa to reappear and, again, circled overhead as they walked home. We often hear tales of dogs following children to school or church but a pigeon?

My most vivid memory of Duke, though, involves Grandpa and her. Grandpa was an active retiree and was often behind the wheel, on his way to visit friends or run errands. Duke would join him, at least for a couple of blocks, and ride on the car's hood like an ornament. Of course, Grandpa drove very slowly, allowing Duke to play hood ornament for as long as possible. It was truly something to see, with children and adults alike pausing to watch them pass. More often than not, the children laughed and pointed while the adults smiled and shook their heads. When Grandpa approached a busy street, he'd rev the engine a bit, signaling to Duke that it was time for her to return home, and off she flew.

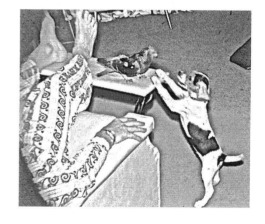

Unfortunately, Duke was taken out late one evening and, in the dark, never made it back home. Although we often asked for another pigeon to raise, none was ever available. In retrospect, I think Grandpa knew that Duke was one of a kind and that no other bird could ever replace her. And today, mention Duke to any of the two-flat's residents and you're sure to get a smile in reply.

MAKING SAUSAGE ... PATTIES

Zia Lea and Sous Chef, Max

For as long as I can remember, the Bartolini Girls made sausage and served them at any meal. They'd cut up a few, add some beaten eggs, and we had a frittata for breakfast. As kids, many is the time we had sausages instead of hot dogs for lunch. For supper the sausages were either served alone, roasted with veggies & potatoes, or cooked in a tomato sauce and served with pasta instead of meatballs. Truth be told, we were much more likely to have sausage than we were to have meat balls. After I moved away, Mom always made sure I had at least one container of frozen sausage patties to take home with me. To this very day, whenever I make sausage, that first whiff of the seasoned ground pork is a trip on a time machine to my youth watching Mom at work. Sure, there are many kinds of sausage available at the local groceries and butchers, not to mention the ethnic markets, but not a one reminds me of home. That's reason enough for me to keep making these.

For you sausage novices, you should know that pork sausage requires a certain amount of fat with some recipes calling for as much as a 25% fat content. This recipe doesn't come near that percentage but fat content is an issue. Never use pork loin for it is far too lean. A pork butt or shoulder roast works best. At one time, I added pork fat to the meat but it took some experimentation to get the right percentage. A few years ago, I decided to try using pancetta. It works perfectly. I add a ½ lb of pancetta to a 4 lb pork butt, grind them together, and my sausage is tasty without too much fat. Better still, it gained Zia's approval.

When you look over our recipe, you'll quickly notice that there is a surprising lack of spices used but, because it's so simple, it can easily be modified to suit your tastes. Mom didn't like fennel seed in her sausage, but I don't think she'd mind if you added some to yours. She didn't like her sausage spicy either, but I'm sure she'd look the other way if you wanted to add some red pepper flakes or a couple shakes of cayenne pepper. I bet Zia would find it interesting if you were to, say, add a little sage or marjoram to the ground meat. Just remember that no matter what spices you use and how much, be sure to start with less than you think necessary and cook a small amount of pork for a taste test. You can always add more if need be.

As for why no sausage links, you may recall that I said earlier that Mom always sent me home with a container of sausage patties and I grew to prefer them. Cooked on the grill, they are a great alternative to hamburgers. Not only that, but a patty or two can be easily crumbled for addition to a tomato sauce, meatloaf, pizza, or some other dish. During one of our Sausage Days, I convinced Zia to just make patties that afternoon and we haven't made a sausage since. If you're a sausage devotee, however, feel free to stuff those casings!

SAUSAGE

INGREDIENTS

6 oz dry white wine

3 cloves garlic, smashed

4 lbs pork butt, coarsely ground

½ lb pancetta, coarsely ground

1½ TBS salt, more or less to taste

2 tsp ground black pepper, more or less to taste

DIRECTIONS

At least 2 hours before beginning, place garlic and wine into a glass and set aside.

Once garlic and wine have "married," combine ground meats and spread in an even layer about 2 inches thick on a work surface.

Season the meat with salt and pepper. Use your fingertips to create dimples in the meat's surface.

Strain the garlic from the wine and discard. Sprinkle the now flavored wine evenly across the meat. Begin mixing the meat until the seasoning and wine are evenly distributed. Create a two inch thick layer with the seasoned meat and let rest for at least 30 minutes so that the flavors meld. (Caution should be taken if you are doing this on a hot summer's day or in a very warm room.)

Once rested, make a mini-patty and cook it in a small frying pan. After tasting, you may need to adjust your seasoning. If you do add seasoning, let it rest 15 minutes before tasting again.

When the sausage meat passes your taste tests, begin making patties. Place them in single layers on baking sheets and into the freezer. Once frozen, you can bag them or place them into containers until needed.

Note: This is one family recipe of many that had never been written down. Mom and Zia had never measured any of the ingredients, other than the meat used. In order to record the recipe, I measured the wine, salt, and pepper before and after the sausage was made. Simple subtraction yielded the amounts shown.

EGGS IN PURGATORY

This simple yet tasty dish can be served for breakfast, lunch, or dinner. Make the sauce from scratch, as I do here, or use a jar of your favorite store-bought. Oh! If ever you're in need of a hangover cure, look no further. This dish is better than the hair of the dog.

INGREDIENTS

2 tbsp olive oil

1 small onion, chopped

1 small clove garlic, minced or grated

red pepper flakes, to taste

1 can (14.5 oz) diced tomatoes

marjoram to taste

salt and pepper

2 large eggs

grated Pecorino Romano cheese for garnish

DIRECTIONS

In a small fry pan with a lid, heat the olive oil over med-high heat.

Add the onions, season with salt and pepper, and sauté until translucent, about 5 minutes.

Add the garlic and red pepper flakes, continue to sauté for about another minute.

Add the tomatoes and marjoram, stir, and bring to a boil before reducing to a soft simmer.

Simmer until the sauce is cooked to your satisfaction. Additional water may be added if the sauce is too dry. Taste to check for seasoning.

Use the back of a ladle or spoon to make an indentation large enough to hold an egg.in the sauce. Fill each with a freshly cracked egg. Try not to break the yolk,

Lightly season the eggs with a bit of salt and pepper, cover, and cook until the eggs are done with the yolks still runny - about 5 minutes.

Serve immediately as-is or atop a slice of Italian bread, garnished with some grated cheese and anything else you may like.

Note: As a rule of thumb, I use one small can of diced tomatoes (14.5 oz) for every 2 eggs being prepared.

MOM'S CHICKEN CACCIATORE

For many hunter-style chicken, *pollo alla cacciatore*, features chicken, pan-braised in a tomato sauce with mushrooms, served over pasta, very often spaghetti. This is not the cacciatore Mom made. Her recipe did not result in a tomato sauce and Mom never served this dish over pasta. I'll leave it to others to decide whether hers was a true cacciatore. I very much prefer her version simply because I've no interest in a chicken-flavored sauce. It doesn't hurt that Mom's dish is delicious. This doesn't mean that tomatoes aren't used in this recipe. I'll add a diced tomato or about a tablespoon of tomato paste "for color," as Mom would say. Additionally, this recipe uses chicken thighs with the skin-on and bone-in because the combination adds so much flavor to the final dish. Of course, you may use whatever chicken parts you wish, with or without skin or bones, but your choices may affect cooking times. Use an instant read thermometer when in doubt. Lastly, if you do not wish to use wine, one cup of chicken broth/stock may be substituted.

INGREDIENTS

2 TBS extra virgin olive oil

3 slices of bacon (or ¼ lb. of pancetta), chopped

5 or 6 chicken thighs, bone-in and skin-on

⅓ cup all-purpose flour

1 large yellow or sweet onion, halved and sliced

3 cloves garlic, sliced

1 bell pepper, cut into strips

8 oz. crimini or button mushrooms, sliced

1 tomato, diced, or 1 TBS tomato paste

2 to 3 TBS fresh rosemary, chopped

1 cup white wine (or low-sodium chicken stock/broth)

2 TBS capers (optional)

3 TBS fresh parsley, chopped, for garnish

salt & pepper, to taste

DIRECTIONS

Heat olive oil in a large frying pan with lid over medium heat.

Add bacon/pancetta and cook until crisp and the fat is rendered. Remove the meat from pan and drain over paper towels. Do not remove the grease from the pan.

Meanwhile, season chicken with salt & pepper. Place flour in a plastic bag, place 2 chicken pieces in the bag, and shake to coat.

Remove chicken to a plate and repeat until all the chicken is coated with flour.

Once the bacon/pancetta has been removed from the frying pan, increase the heat to med-high and add the chicken pieces, skin-side down. Sauté until chicken is lightly browned, about 5 – 6 minutes. Turn the chicken pieces over, and sauté until they, too, are lightly browned — another 5 minutes or so.

Remove chicken and reserve.

Discard all but about 3 TBS of fat from the frying pan. Add the onion and begin sautéing. Lightly season with salt & pepper.

Use a wooden spoon to clean the pan's bottom of the brown bits. (This is where the flavor is.)

After about 5 minutes, add the garlic and bell peppers and continue sautéing .

After 5 minutes more, add the mushrooms.

5 minutes later, add the tomato/paste and sauté for 2 – 3 minutes. Season lightly with salt & pepper.

Return the bacon/pancetta to the pan. Season with the rosemary. Return the chicken to the pan and add the wine.

Bring the pan to the boil before covering and reducing heat to medium-low.

Continue cooking for 45 minutes or until chicken is fully cooked. (Use an instant read thermometer if in doubt.) Periodically, throughout the cooking, slightly shift the chicken pieces to prevent their sticking/burning. If the pan looks too dry, add a little water or chicken broth. Chicken is ready when it reaches 165° F.

A few minutes before serving, sprinkle the capers over the pan's contents (optional).

Taste the sauce to see if salt or pepper is needed.

When finished cooking, remove to a serving platter and garnish with parsley.

Note: The cacciatore may be served as-is or over a bed of polenta, buttered noodles, rice, or couscous.

MOM'S OSSO BUCO

This dish was listed twice in Mom's notebooks, the first being little more than a few notes. This recipe is the more complete version and is a delicious preparation. Although I've adapted the recipe to use a slow cooker, instruction for cooking the shanks using an oven follow the recipe. Don't overlook the gremolata. It's unique, requiring minced anchovies, and is a wonderful garnish for the shanks.

Note: It is possible to purchase veal today that has been more humanely raised than has been in the past. It is expensive, however. If you wish to prepare this dish but without veal for whatever reason, beef shanks are a suitable substitution -- and far less expensive.

INGREDIENTS

FOR THE OSSO BUCO

4 veal shanks about 2 inches thick
salt and pepper
⅓ cup all-purpose flour
2 to 3 TBS olive oil
1 large onion sliced
1 carrot, chopped
1 celery stalk, chopped
2 cloves garlic, sliced

1 large can (28 oz) whole tomatoes, torn/crushed by hand
2 TBS tomato paste
1 bay leaf
½ cup dry white wine
½ cup veal stock – chicken may be substituted

FOR THE GREMOLATA

2 anchovy fillets, minced — 1 tsp anchovy paste may be substituted
1 garlic clove, minced
3 TBS fresh parsley, chopped
zest of 1 lemon

DIRECTIONS

Season the shanks with salt & pepper on both sides. Begin to heat some oil in a frying pan over medium heat.

Place about ⅓ cup of flour into a plastic bag, followed by 2 of the shanks.

Carefully shake to coat the shanks with flour.

Place the shanks in the now hot oil and repeat with the remaining 2 flanks.

Cook the shanks until both sides are browned, – about 7 or 8 minutes total. Remove and reserve.

Meanwhile, add the onions, garlic, carrots, celery, tomatoes, tomato paste, and bay leaf to the slow cooker. Season liberally with salt and pepper. Stir until combined.

Use the white wine to deglaze the frying pan and pour the liquid into the slow cooker when finished.

Add the shanks to the slow cooker. Be sure to include any of the juices that may have collected on the plate.

Add enough stock so that the sauce comes halfway up the sides of the shanks.

Set the slow cooker to "LOW" and cook for 8 hours. To speed up the cooking time, for every hour cooked on "HIGH" reduce the cooking time by 2 hours.

About every 2 hours, baste the top of the shanks to keep them moist.

Towards the end of the cooking process, prepare the gremolata by combining the anchovies, garlic, parsley, and zest in a small bowl. Stir until fully combined.

Carefully remove the shanks and serve immediately with sauce and garnished with a sprinkling of gremolata.

Note: To cook shanks in the oven

Preheat the oven to 350° F.

Increase the amount of liquids use ⅔ cups dry white wine and ¾ cups stock.

Use a dutch oven and cook for 1½ to 2 hours. Meat should be fork tender and just about falling off the bone. Let it go too long and it will fall of the bone, ruining your presentation.

PORCHETTA

Traditionally, porchetta meant the roasting of an entire pig. In fact, one such pig was roasted at a neighborhood bakery and served at the wedding reception of Zia Lea and Uncle Al. (Imagine a time when a neighborhood bakery used their oven to roast your pig.) Although roasting a pig may be fine when feeding large groups, a pig roast is out of the question for most families. My family, like many, used the pig's foreleg, a picnic ham, for the roast. The meat was butterflied, removing the bone in the process, and then heavily seasoned with, among other things, fennel fronds which are similar to dill in both appearance and taste. The result was a juicy roast, with herbal flavoring throughout. Times have changed and picnic hams aren't as readily available as they once were. Our family switched to roasting bone-in pork loins initially but as time passed, they, too, became less available and we began roasting boneless pork loins. Although still very good, nothing beats the flavor of a roasted leg of pork.

INGREDIENTS

4 TBS fennel fronds, chopped
4 TBS fresh parsley, chopped
8 to 10 garlic cloves, diced
3 to 4 TBS fresh rosemary, chopped
olive oil
1 raw picnic shoulder ham, skin on, bone
  removed, butterflied
salt and pepper
1 TBS marjoram
12 whole garlic cloves

1 fennel bulb, thinly sliced
1 onion, thinly sliced
3 celery stalks, chopped
3 carrots, cut into large pieces
fingerlings or new potatoes
3 rosemary sprigs
6 cups chicken stock, divided
3 cups dry white wine, divided
3 TBS all-purpose flour
butter

DIRECTIONS

About an hour before the porchetta is to go into the oven, combine the fennel fronds, parsley, chopped garlic, and rosemary. Add enough olive oil to make a paste, stir, and set aside.

Use a sharp knife to score the pork skin, making a checkerboard or diamond pattern. Try to avoid cutting deeply into the pork meat, if at all.

Place the roast, skin-side down, and "open it" to expose as much of the roast's inside surface area as possible.

Evenly coat the exposed flesh with the herbal paste created in the first step. Season with marjoram before liberally seasoning with salt & pepper.

Roll the roast and use twine to securely tie it. Set roast aside while it loses its chill.

In a roasting pan, add the sliced onions, fennel, celery, and whole garlic cloves. Season liberally with salt & pepper.

Place the roast atop the bed of roasting vegetables. Pre-heat oven to 450° F.

Coat the roast with olive oil, add 2 cups stock plus 1 cup wine to the roasting pan.

Place roasting pan in pre-heated oven. Every 20 minutes, baste the roast with the pan juices, add more stock and wine to the pan, if needed. (Be sure to reserve 2 cups of stock and ½ cup of wine for use later.)

Meanwhile, place potatoes and carrots into a large bowl, season with salt and pepper, some rosemary, and enough olive oil to coat. Mix well.

After 60 minutes total time, reduce oven temperature to 325° F, baste the roast adding more liquid to the pan if needed, and place the seasoned carrots and potatoes into the roasting pan.

(continued)

From this point forward, continue to baste the roast every 30 minutes or so, replenishing the pan juices when necessary. If outer skin grows too brown, use aluminum foil to tent the porchetta.

The roast will be finished when the internal temperature reaches 160° F. When ready, remove the roast to a cutting board and tent with aluminum foil to rest for at least 15 minutes. Remove the carrots and potatoes to a covered bowl. Strain the pan juices from remaining stewing vegetables.

Use the reserved ½ cup of wine to deglaze the roasting pan over high heat.

Use a grease separator to remove all but 3 TBS of grease from the strained liquid.

Reduce heat to medium, add the 3 TBS of grease to the roasting pan, and add 3 tbs all-purpose flour. Mix thoroughly and cook for a minute or so to create a roux.

Add the remaining pan juice liquids and stir until the sauce begins to thicken.

Begin adding the reserved stock to the pan, stirring constantly, over medium heat.

Once all the stock has been added and the sauce thickened, taste for seasoning, remove from heat, and add a tab of butter to finish the sauce.

Before carving the roast, use a small knife to remove the skin (crackling), which may be served with the roast or left in the kitchen as the Cook's reward.

Slice and serve the roast, accompanied by the sauce and reserved roasted vegetables.

Grandpa and His Much-Prized Model A

HERB-ROASTED DUCK

When I was very young, frozen foods were just becoming widely available. My parents bought a large chest freezer, placed it in our basement, and both families used it to store foods. As the years passed, we kids grew older and oftentimes we wouldn't be home for dinner. With Dad working at the restaurant, Mom sometimes ate alone. On one such night, Zia invited Mom to join them for dinner. She had roasted a duck! Mom gratefully accepted and everyone sitting at the table commented how delicious the duck was. At some point, Mom asked her Sister what possessed her to roast a duck in mid-week. Was she celebrating something? No, Zia had been looking in the freezer that morning for dinner ideas, saw the duck, and decided to roast it. That's when Mom realized that Zia, that dear sweet woman we all know and love, was a duck thief. She had stolen Mom's duck!

This is a delicious way to roast duck or any fowl, for that matter. I wouldn't suggest stealing the bird, though.

INGREDIENTS

1 duck, approx 6 lbs, rinsed and dried, neck and giblets removed
a few sprigs of thyme and rosemary, with a few whole sage leaves
½ onion, cut into quarters
½ lemon, cut into quarters
4 garlic cloves, smashed
zest of ½ lemon
fresh thyme, rosemary, and sage leaves, chopped, 3 TBS total
olive oil

DIRECTIONS

Pre-heat oven to 350° F

Season the duck's cavities with salt and pepper.

Place one garlic clove in the neck cavity and the remaining garlic, onion, and lemon into the abdominal cavity, along with the sage leaves and sprigs of rosemary and thyme. Use kitchen twine to tie the legs. Fold the wing tips under the duck's back.

To aid in draining the fat, use a skewer or similarity pointed object to pierce the duck breasts repeatedly. Coat lightly with olive oil and lightly season the breast side of the duck with salt and pepper.

Place the duck on the roasting rack, breast side down.

Coat lightly with olive oil and liberally season the back with salt, pepper, and ⅓ of the chopped herbs.

Place in the pre-heated oven for 30 minutes. Remove from oven, turn duck so it is now breast-side up, season with remaining herbs, and return to oven.

Roast for 90 minutes, basting every 30 minutes.

After final basting, raise oven temp to 375° F for another 30 minutes to crisp the skin.

Let rest for 15 minutes before carving.

SIDES & SALADS
CONTORNI E INSALATE

Mom and Zia Lea, aged 2 and 4 years old

GRANDMA'S CHICKEN GIZZARDS WITH PEAS

Mom and Zia were little girls when the Great Depression struck and our family, like so many others, was hit hard. By all accounts, these were lean times. Our Grandpa struggled to provide for his family. Both Bartolini Girls marvel(ed) at how Grandma could make a single chicken last a full week, feeding a family of four in the process. Well, that's when she could get a chicken. This recipe comes from that time and Mom often served it when I was growing up.

INGREDIENTS

5 or 6 oz chicken gizzards & hearts,
    cleaned and trimmed
1 small onion, divided in halves
water
1 TBS olive oil

2 TBS butter
1 plum tomato, chopped
2 cups frozen or fresh peas
pinch of cloves
salt and pepper, to taste

DIRECTIONS

Place gizzards, half of the onion, and enough lightly salted water to cover into a medium saucepan. Cover, bring to a boil over med-high heat, and reduce to a soft simmer.

Softly simmer for 1 hour, checking periodically to ensure enough water remains. At the end of an hour, pour the pan's contents through a strainer, discarding the onion and stewing liquid.

Slice the remaining onion portion and roughly chop the stewed meat.

In the same pan, heat oil and butter over medium high heat.

Return gizzards to the pan, along with the sliced onion, and sauté until the onion is soft and translucent.

Add tomato and sauté for a minute before adding peas, cloves, and a few TBS of water to the pan. Season with salt and pepper, cover, and cook about 5 minutes or until peas are done to you liking.

Serve immediately.

GRANDPA'S TUNA SALAD

At noon on any given Friday, save those that fell in the worst of winter, you could find Grandpa in the patio enjoying his lunch. It was usually a simple dish and, being Catholic, it was also meat-free. A favorite of Grandpa, and later my own, was this simple tuna salad. Believe me, it could not get any more simple and no further introduction is required.

INGREDIENTS

1 can (5 oz) chunk tuna, packed in olive
oil, well-drained
a bit of red onion, thinly sliced
2 whole anchovy fillets, more if desired
olive oil
red wine vinegar
salt & pepper, to taste

DIRECTIONS

Place the tuna on a serving plate. It can be flaked or left in a ring shape.

Top with onion and anchovies.

Sprinkle with olive oil and red wine vinegar.

Season with salt, & pepper, to taste

Serve with crusty bread and a glass of (homemade) white wine.

BACCALÀ SALAD

This salad is a light, colorful way to prepare baccalà. Many Italian families serve it on Christmas Eve but it is just as welcome at a summer's supper. You'll find that, no matter when it's served, this salad will brighten any table.

INGREDIENTS

1 lb baccalà, well-rinsed - p 129
pickled bell peppers, chopped - optional
½ yellow bell pepper, chopped
1 celery stalk, chopped
some red onion chopped
nonpareil capers, rinsed

Kalamata olives, halved
¼ cup fresh parsley, chopped
extra virgin olive oil
red wine vinegar — lemon juice may be
    substituted
salt & pepper, to taste

DIRECTIONS

Clean the rinsed baccalà of any bones and skin.

Bring a large pot of water to the boil.

Meanwhile, cut the baccalà into pieces from 3 to 4 inches apiece.

When the water is boiling hard, add the baccalà. When the water returns to the boil, reduce the heat to a soft simmer.

Simmer until the baccalà can be easily flaked, usually about 5 to 8 minutes.

Using a slotted spoon or small strainer, remove the baccalà from the water and set aside.

Once cool, carefully flake the baccalà and place in another bowl along with the peppers, celery, onion, capers, olives, and parsley. Gently toss the ingredients until combined.

Add enough of the olive oil to lightly coat the salad, followed by the vinegar/lemon juice to taste. Season with pepper but be sure to taste before adding any salt.

If not served immediately, cover and refrigerate until you're ready to do so.

MOM'S CAPONATA

Originating in Sicily, caponata is now served throughout much of Italy in a variety of forms. All versions have eggplant as the dish's star ingredient, along with olive oil, onions, tomato, and garlic. To that base, bell peppers, mushrooms, olives, pine nuts, (*pignoli*), and even fish have been added to this tasty side dish. The selection of the additional components depends as much upon the individual cook as it does the region of Italy. There's no better example of this than Mom's recipe and the one that Zia Lea, her sister, follows. Both included some bell pepper and mushrooms but Mom also added zucchini; Zia rarely, if ever, does. The difference here is minimal but, then again, their kitchens were only separated by less than 20 vertical feet. Imagine the differences when there's hundreds of miles separating the kitchens. Still more important than which recipe to follow is finding the right ingredients. Like Mom & Zia, I'll choose only those vegetables that are fresh and "in season" for best results.

INGREDIENTS

3 TBS olive oil
1 medium onion, halved and sliced
1 bell pepper, sliced into strips
2 cloves garlic, minced
1 doz button or crimini mushrooms,
    quartered

3 TBS freshly chopped parsley
1 zucchini, cubed
2 or 3 medium eggplants, cubed -
    peeling optional
2 plum tomatoes, cubed
salt & pepper, to taste

DIRECTIONS

Add oil to a large fry pan and heat over a med-high heat.

Add onion and bell pepper, season with salt & pepper, and sauté until barely soft, about 5 minutes.

Add garlic and sauté for 1 minute.

Add mushrooms and continue sautéing for about 5 minutes.

Add eggplant, zucchini, tomatoes, and parsley, stir to combine, season with salt and pepper, and sauté until done to your liking, at least 8 minutes more.

The dish is now done and may be served hot, warm, or at room temperature.

Note: Leftover caponata can be used to dress pasta or, my favorite, in an omelet or frittata.

MOM'S CALAMARI SALAD

There are a number of explanations for the origins of the Feast of the Seven Fishes on Christmas Eve. Some say it is an entirely Italian-American tradition, while others claim it originated in Sicily. Many say the number is based on the 7 Sacraments of the Christian Faith. That may be true but it doesn't explain another version of the Feast that includes 13 seafood dishes. Could they represent the 12 Apostles and Christ? Perhaps, but what about those who celebrate with feasts of 8, 10, or even 11 fishes? We'll probably never know.

What we do know is that prior to the changes brought by Vatican Council II in the 1960s, Christmas Eve was a "fast & abstain" day in the Catholic Church. That meant only one main meal could be consumed and no meat was to be eaten all day. Serving a seafood feast as the day's only meal was a way to adhere to the Church's policies and still celebrate the imminent birth of the Christ Child.

Though we didn't celebrate the Feast of the Seven Fishes, we did enjoy a seafood dinner on Christmas Eve. One of the dishes Mom served was a simple salad made with calamari, bell peppers, and onion. This is another colorful salad that will brighten any table, no matter when it's served.

INGREDIENTS

squid, cleaned and cut into rings   *extra virgin olive oil*
          (halve tentacles, if using)   *lemon juice*
green bell pepper, diced   *fresh parsley*
red bell pepper, diced   *salt & pepper, to taste*

DIRECTIONS

Fill a large saucepan with water and bring to a rolling boil over high heat.

Add the calamari, stir, and turn off the heat.

After one minute remove the calamari and place in an ice bath to chill. (Calamari may be held here for a couple of hours until ready to be served.)

Once fully chilled, drain, place calamari on paper towels, and pat dry before adding to a bowl containing the diced salad ingredients.

Dress immediately with lemon juice, olive oil, parsley, salt and pepper. Toss and serve immediately or refrigerate until ready to do so.

Note: When cooking calamari, either cook it a little - one minute - or a lot - 45 minutes. Anything in-between will result in rubbery calamari.

THE BARTOLINI GIRLS' BEET SALAD

Everyone has one — or maybe two or three. A go-to recipe used when an occasion calls for you to bring a dish. Today's recipe is one that Mom and my Zia often used to fulfill their potluck obligation. To be honest, I've no idea who first discovered this recipe. I remember Mom serving it for dinner during my childhood and Zia brings it to dinners to this very day. A colorful dish, this is much lighter than potato salad and is sure to be a hit among beet lovers. You'll note that I roast the beets before using. If you've neither the time nor inclination for roasting beets, most groceries stock a variety of beets sold in jars, any of which will make fine substitutes.

There are no amounts given because much depends upon the size of the serving dish. Use as much of each ingredient as needed to create a colorful layered salad.

INGREDIENTS

raw beets, washed with greens trimmed
diced onion
mayonnaise
eggs, hard-boiled and chopped
salt & pepper to taste
sweet paprika for garnish, optional

DIRECTIONS

TO PREPARE THE BEETS

Pre-heat oven to 400° F.

Place the beets in a roasting pan or on a baking sheet. Drizzle with olive oil, season with salt, and place in the middle of the oven. Roast for 30 to 40 minutes, depending upon the size of the beets. The beets are fully roasted when a knife's blade meets little resistance when the largest beet is pierced. Set aside to cool.

Once cool enough to handle, use a paring knife to trim the beets' tops and bottoms. Much of the skin of each bulb should slip off easily. Use a paring knife to remove the rest.

Use a knife, food processor, or mandolin to dice, shred, or slice the beets. Set aside.

Note: If store-bought beets are used, just drain them and proceed with the recipe below

TO ASSEMBLE THE SALAD

Place beets in a serving dish. Mom created a layer about an inch deep. Season lightly with salt.

Sprinkle a couple of tablespoons of diced onion on top of the beets. Use more or less depending upon the onion's strength.

Add enough mayonnaise to completely cover the ingredients.

Use the chopped, hard-boiled eggs to top off the salad.

Season with salt, pepper, and garnish with sweet paprika.

Chill fully before serving.

CACIONI

Common to much of Italy, cacioni are small, half-moon shaped pies which Mom filled with a combination of Swiss chard and spinach. In Italy, you can find them filled with a variety of cheeses and, in one case, even beans. Up until relatively recently, our cacioni were always fried but that changed one afternoon when Zia had lunch with her *Sammarinese* friends. One of the women shared cacioni that had been baked, and that was a game-changer. Now, cacioni could be made and frozen for later use, unlike those made for frying. No matter which way you prepare them, cacioni make a tasty and interesting side dish.

These little pies were a big hit in our family. Mom had a devil of a time keeping us kids away from those that she had just cooked. We were sure to grab one as we passed by the stove if she was at all distracted. With three of us "innocently" walking through her kitchen, those cacioni never did stand a chance. It was a wonder any actually made it to the dinner table.

INGREDIENTS

FOR THE DOUGH

Mom's pasta dough - p 26

FOR THE FILLING

3 TBS olive oil
2 cloves garlic, crushed
1 small yellow onion, chopped
1 large bunch fresh Swiss chard,
       trimmed, leaves chopped after
       removal from stalks, stalks
       chopped and reserved

½ pkg frozen chopped spinach, thawed
    — more or less, to taste
salt & pepper to taste

DIRECTIONS

Heat oil and garlic in a frying pan over medium heat until garlic begins to brown, about 5 minutes. Do not allow garlic to burn.

Remove garlic, increase heat to med-high, add onion and as much of the chopped chard stalks as you prefer. Season with salt & pepper and sauté until the onion is translucent, about 8 minutes.

Add chopped spinach to pan and continue sautéing until heated through, about 4 minutes.

Add chard leaves, season with salt & pepper, and sauté until leaves are wilted and cooked to your preference.

Place cooked greens in a colander or strainer, place a dish on top of the cooked vegetables, and place a heavy can or similar weight on top of the dish. This will help to drain as much liquid from the greens as possible before filling the cacioni.

(continued)

TO MAKE FRIED CACIONI

INGREDIENTS

Mom's pasta dough - p 26 - rested for 30 minutes after preparation
Swiss chard with spinach, sautéed and well-drained
oil for frying

DIRECTIONS

Separate dough into quarters and wrap 3 quarters in plastic wrap.

Using the remaining dough quarter, run it repeatedly through the pasta machine rollers until thin. If no. 1 is the widest setting, continue rolling the dough up to, and including, the no. 6 position.

Spread the dough sheet on a flat surface. Using a bowl, saucer, or widemouthed mug/jar as a template, cut circles as large as you can on the dough sheet. Trim and reserve the excess dough for later use.

Depending upon the size of the dough circle, place 2 to 4 TBS of the chard filling in a line across the center of each one. Using a pastry brush or your finger tips, lightly moisten the edge of each circle with water. Fold the pastry in half upon itself, creating a half-moon. Use a fork to press and seal the edges of the dough.

Use the fork to prick each pie once to allow steam to escape during frying. Set aside. Continue until all the filling has been used. The left-over dough may be used to make the pasta of your choosing. (Mom made quadretti, p - 38.)

Using a large frying pan, add enough vegetable/peanut oil to create a depth of 1 to 1½ inches. To avoid boiling over, do not fill the pan over halfway full. (This is more a "shallow-fry" than deep-fry. Of course, if you prefer deep-frying, go for it.)

Bring oil to 360° F. Depending upon the pan size, fry 2, 3, or 4 cacioni at a time. Do not overcrowd. Fry until golden brown before turning each one over.

Place a wire rack atop a baking sheet and place both into a warm oven. When each batch of cacioni are finished frying, place them on the rack in the oven to keep warm. Sprinkle with coarse kosher or sea salt.

Repeat the process until all are fried. Serve immediately.

TO MAKE BAKED CACIONI

INGREDIENTS

> *Enough of your favorite homemade or store-bought pastry dough - not puff pastry - to make a double-crusted pie.*
> *Swiss chard with spinach, sautéed and well-drained*
> *1 egg yolk mixed with a TBS of water to make a wash*

DIRECTIONS

Roll the dough as thin as you would for a pie crust.

Using a bowl, saucer, or wide-mouthed mug/jar as a template, cut circles as large as you can on the dough sheet. Trim and reserve the excess dough for later use.

Depending upon the size of the dough circle, place 2 to 4 TBS of the chard filling in a line across the center of each one. Using a pastry brush or your finger tips, moisten the edge of each circle with water. Fold the pastry in half upon itself, creating a half-moon. Use a fork to press and seal the edges of the dough.

Use the fork to prick each pie to allow steam to escape during baking. Set aside on a baking sheet lined with parchment paper.

Continue until no more dough remains and then place the baking sheet into the fridge while you work with the second half of the pastry dough. Repeat the process until there is no more filling or dough.

(continued)

IF BAKING IMMEDIATELY

DIRECTIONS

Pre-heat oven to 375 F.°

Meanwhile, chill the cacioni for a few minutes before proceeding. This will help to make the pastry even more crispy.

Using a pastry brush, carefully coat the exposed surface of each pie with the egg wash. Sprinkle with salt.

Place baking sheet into pre-heated oven and bake until golden brown, about 20 minutes.

Serve immediately.

TO FREEZE AND BAKE LATER

DIRECTIONS

Place newly prepared cacioni on a lined baking sheet and then into the freezer.

After a couple of hours, place the cacioni into more permanent freezer containers.

When ready to cook, DO NOT THAW. Pre-heat oven to 350° F.

Remove the cacioni from the freezer, place on a parchment-lined baking sheet, and, using a pastry brush, coat the exposed surface of each pie with egg wash. Sprinkle with coarse kosher or sea salt.

Place the baking sheet into a pre-heated oven and bake until golden brown, 30 to 40 minutes.

Serve immediately.

Grandma Erselia (c 1928)

DAD AND HIS DANDELIONS

When the lawns started to green each spring, the adults in the two-flat became wild chicory and dandelion pickers. Depending upon our age, we kids also took part. When very young, Mom & Zia would take us to some park where we'd play as they "harvested" the tender, young dandelions growing about. A couple of years would pass and we would be considered old enough to join in on the fun. We were each given our own butter knife, shown how to cut the greens out of the ground, and taught to leave the area if "traces" of dog were spotted. So, off we proudly went, with knife in one hand and an Easter basket in the other. That's right. Our Easter baskets were repurposed each spring and used to carry the harvest.

Now Dad loved his dandelions. Sis & I often went with him, spending Sunday mornings after Mass picking dandelions. We loved every minute of it — until we were around 8 or 9 years of age. It was about then when we learned that not all kids spent Sunday mornings picking dandelions. In fact, we were the only ones to do so. Peer pressure being what it was, we began to balk at the idea of spending Sunday mornings picking weeds. Did that stop Dad?

Not in the slightest. Dad's love of dandelions knew little of, nor cared about, peer pressure. If anything, Dad's peers probably encouraged him to get out there and pick those greens. For Sis and I, it wasn't so much that he picked the greens, it was when and where he chose to do so. You see, the old two-flat was on the same block as the parish church and about a half mile from both was a freeway. Having attended an early morning Mass, Sis and I would jump into the back seat of the car and off we'd go with Dad as he ran errands and stopped for "un caffè" with friends or family. That first part of the ride was fraught with anxiety for Sis and I. If Dad turned left at the Church, we were fine. It's when he turned right that we began to get nervous — and it grew worse as we approached the freeway. If he turned anywhere before the overpass, we breathed a sigh of relief and all was well. The same held true if we drove over and beyond the bridge. It was only when we heard his turn indicator as we drove on the overpass that we knew we were heading for the freeway and trouble! "Please, Dad, NO!" As soon as he made the left turn, Dad pulled the car onto the entrance ramp's shoulder, no more than 10 feet from the corner. There, in full view of our fellow parishioners — and classmates — walking to-and-from Sunday Mass, Dad pulled out his penknife & paper bag and started picking weeds, while Sis and I, mortified, dove for cover in the back seat. How could he do this to us! Two forevers later, he'd return to the car and off we'd go to the park where the pickings would be better, or so Dad said. We didn't care. We just wanted out of there.

Looking back, and hindsight being what it is, I'm pretty sure that Dad stopped along that ramp for more than just some dandelion greens. To begin with, Dad was a practical joker and he probably stood outside of the car and laughed as we tried to hide ourselves in the back seat. Although at the time it seemed like an eternity, we were actually parked there for only a few minutes and Dad never returned with more than a few greens, if any. No, we always needed to go to the park afterward and, suddenly, Sis and I were more than happy to accompany and even help him, proving there'd be no need to ever stop on that ramp again. As a result, we had all the greens Dad needed in no time flat and soon we were on our way to our next stop.

Yeah, we got played!

DANDELION SALAD

Where some eat dandelions in all stages of growth, we only ate the youngest of plants. This meant that spring was dandelion season for us pickers. Once picked and cleaned, we prepare them in a very simple salad, as you're about to see.

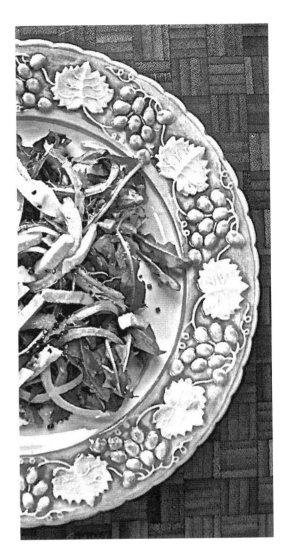

INGREDIENTS

*fresh dandelion leaves, washed and
          trimmed, and patted dry*
sliced onion
hard boiled eggs, chopped
olive oil
red wine vinegar

DIRECTIONS

Place the dandelions, onion, and egg into a salad bowl. Add olive oil and vinegar, season with salt and pepper, toss gently, and serve.

Note: When harvesting wild plants, be sure to avoid areas that have been sprayed with any kind of chemical treatment. If in doubt, choose another locale.

FRIED CALAMARI

Prior to developing this recipe a few years ago, I experimented using batters to coat the calamari rings, as well as soaking some in buttermilk. I found that a buttermilk soak and a coating of seasoned flour produced the tastiest and crispiest calamari -- and I haven't ordered fried calamari in a restaurant since.

INGREDIENTS

*1 lb. squid (about 16 medium-sized),
     cleaned and cut into ½ inch
     rings (Frozen, raw rings may be
     substituted. Thaw before using.)
2 cups buttermilk
1 cup all-purpose flour
1 TBS garlic powder
½ tsp coarse kosher or sea salt
1 tsp cayenne pepper – more or less to
     taste
¼ tsp pepper
vegetable oil for frying*

DIRECTIONS

Place buttermilk, calamari rings, and tentacles into a bowl and set aside for one hour. If longer, refrigerate until you're ready.

Heat oil in a large sauce pan or dutch oven over med-high heat.

Place dry ingredients into a bowl and whisk to combine.

Line a sheet pan with paper towels and pre-heat oven to 200° F.

When oil reaches 360° F. remove some pieces of calamari from the buttermilk and allow excess liquid to run off before dredging them in the flour mixture.

Place pieces, one at a time, into the hot oil. Work in batches. Do not overcrowd. Flip to cook all sides.

Remove calamari when golden brown, about 90 seconds to 2 minutes, and place on paper-lined sheet pan. Sprinkle with salt and place in warmed oven.

When all are fried, serve immediately with lemon wedges and your favorite dipping sauce.

GRANDMA'S STUFFED VEGETABLES

August was a good month for the Bartolini Clan at the two-flat. Grandpa's garden was in high-gear, easily producing enough tomatoes for both families' needs. (Be sure to check out Mom's Tomato Antipasti - p 208.) As the years passed, the garden grew and so did the selection of produce. Lettuce, Swiss chard, eggplants, peppers, and, of course, grapes all made their way onto our dinner tables in August. To augment his own crops, Grandpa and I made a weekly trip to Detroit's Eastern Market every Saturday morning where he would walk the aisles, haggling each farmer/vendor over the price of whatever it was that he wanted to buy. By the end of our tour, we'd return to the car with everything from fruits & vegetables to chickens (dead or alive) and, one memorable Saturday each year, a hog's head to be made into head cheese. You've not lived until you've walked around a crowded farmers market carrying a hog's head on your shoulder, stopping occasionally while your Grandfather haggled with some farmer over what amounted to 25 cents, if that. Sunday nights, both families often dined together on the patio, which Grandpa had built adjacent to the garage. It easily accommodated the 12 of us and very often a few guests more.

These dinners went off like a well-oiled machine. While Dad, Uncle, and Grandpa worked the grill and their beverages, Mom and Zia handled the rest, from setting the table to making sure that the "trouble-makers" among us 6 kids sat at opposite ends of the long table. Once, in anticipation of this seating arrangement, walkie talkies were snuck into the patio. Though clever, the tactic was extremely short-lived. Our parents took away the devices before the first "Roger wilco!" was uttered.

Once everyone was seated, all were treated to a wonderful meal, often featuring side dishes made from the garden's vegetables. Family favorites were tomatoes, eggplant, and onions that were halved, topped with our breading mixture, and baked. Both Mom and Zia spoke of Grandma preparing vegetables in this way, which is similar to recipes for Tomatoes Provençal. Surprisingly, when I last visited San Marino, Zia Pina served them as part of my welcoming dinner. These vegetables are not only a great side dish but they make incredibly good sandwiches for lunch the following day.

INGREDIENTS

small onions, top and bottom
      removed, halved and
      the inner flesh scored
      with a knife tip
eggplants, halved and the
      inner flesh scored
      with a knife tip
tomatoes, halved, with some
      of the juice squeezed
      into the breading
      mixture
enough of the Bartolini
      breading - p 22 - to
      amply cover the
      halved vegetables
olive oil
salt & pepper

DIRECTIONS

Pre-heat oven to 400° F.

Lightly oil a baking sheet or dish and place the onions on the dish, scored side up. Drizzle with olive oil and season with salt and pepper. (Trim the ends so that the onions won't roll.)

Bake the onions, alone, for 20 minutes. Remove and lower the oven temperature to 350° F.

Place the rest of the vegetables on the baking sheet/tray, drizzle with olive oil, and season lightly with salt and pepper.

Cover each half with the breading mixture and then add another light drizzle of olive oil.

Bake for 40 to 45 minutes. Serve immediately.

Remember: Save a tomato or eggplant for a sandwich you'll enjoy the following day.

SWEETS
DOLCI

Justin, Paul, Sr

Paul, Jr, Dionne Michael Rhonda

MOM'S BISCOTTI WITH PECANS

Like many households the Thanksgiving to New Year's Day holiday season at our house was a special time each year, complete with its own set of dishes and treats. These biscotti fit into that group although I don't know why. It's not as if they're festive-looking, like sugar cookies decorated to look like Santa or Christmas trees. Nor are they part of some widely accepted food tradition such as eggnog at Christmas or turkey on Thanksgiving. Yet the first of these biscotti would quietly make their appearance in our homes sometime around Thanksgiving and, come January, they would leave just as quietly. To this very day, Zia gives each of us some biscotti sometime during the holidays — and it wouldn't be Christmas without them.

This first recipe is the one Mom would prepare. It came from family friends that Dad knew back in the Old Country. We estimate it to be well over 100 years old. It's a great dunking cookie, one we kids loved.

INGREDIENTS

1 lb powdered sugar
½ cup granulated sugar
¾ lb butter, softened
8 eggs
lemon zest from at least 2 lemons
2 heaping tsp baking soda
9 cups all-purpose flour, sifted
whole pecans - walnuts may be substituted

DIRECTIONS

At medium speed, beat sugars and butter together until very light. Add eggs, one at a time, and continue beating until well-blended.

At low-speed, add the lemon zest and baking soda. Gradually add the flour and mix well. The resultant dough will be pretty stiff.

Divide the dough into 6 equal portions. Roll each into a rectangular shape, about 12 inches long and 6 inches inches wide.

Line the center of each with the pecans and fold up the ends to cover the nuts, forming loaves that are about 11 inches long by 3 to 4 inches wide. Do not over-fill with pecans because the loaves will crumble when you slice them later.

Place the loaves on greased, floured baking sheets and bake in a pre-heated 350° F oven for 30 minutes. Slice them while warm or they'll crumble if you wait too long.

If you prefer to have the biscotti toasted, remove them from the oven after they have become a pale golden brown, usually in 15 to 20 minutes. Slice them, place them on their side, and return them to the oven for an additional 10 to 15 minutes. Turn them over midway through the cooking time.

ZIA LEA'S ANISE-FLAVORED BISCOTTI

This is Zia's biscotti recipe. She started preparing them about the same time I was born, some 25 years ago, give or take a few decades. The anise flavoring was a bit strong for us kids but it was a favorite of the adults.

Every year, the two Sisters made a batch of their respective biscotti and then traded half with each other. Both houses ended up with enough biscotti to last the holidays, with adults and children being satisfied.

INGREDIENTS

5 cups of all-purpose flour, sifted
½ tsp salt
4 tsp baking soda
½ tsp baking powder

2 cup granulated sugar
½ cup butter, softened
6 eggs
2 TBS anise extract

DIRECTIONS

Sift flour, salt, baking soda and powder together. Set aside.

In another bowl, beat butter with sugar on medium speed till creamy. Add eggs one at a time. When finished, add the anise flavoring.

Slowly add flour mixture and beat at low-speed till well-blended. If the dough feels too stiff, add an extra dab of butter.

Divide mixture into quarters. Form a loaf from each quarter and place 2 loaves on each baking sheet. Bake in a pre-heated 350° F oven for 30 minutes. Slice them while warm; they'll crumble if you wait too long.

If you prefer to have the biscotti toasted, remove them from the oven after they have become a pale golden brown — usually in 15 to 20 minutes. Slice them, place them on their side, and return them to the oven for an additional 10 to 15 minutes. Turn them over midway through the cooking time.

FIOCCHETTI

Fiocchetti are a sweet treat that Mom would make for us kids on occasion. I've since learned they are a popular item throughout Italy during Mardi Gras, *Carnivale*. Depending upon where you are in Italy, fiocchetti may be called: *chiacchiere*, *manzòle*, *bugie*, or *risole*. No matter what you call them, basically, they're all the same: thin strips of sweetened dough that are deep-fried and coated with sugar. You can probably guess why Mom only made them for us "on occasion".

INGREDIENTS

2 cups all-purpose flour, plus as
    much as ¼ cup more
2 whole eggs
2 egg yolks

2 TBS rum - white wine may be
    used - optional
3 TBS confectioners sugar
⅛ tsp salt
oil for frying

DIRECTIONS

Mix together all ingredients except oil and combine as if making pasta and form a large ball. (You can do this in a food processor, if you like.)

Put ¼ cup flour on work surface and knead dough, using as much of the flour as necessary to create a smooth and shiny dough. This should take about 10 minutes.

Cover in plastic wrap and refrigerate for at least one hour.

Roll out dough until very thin. (A pasta machine can be used to roll out the dough.) Cut the dough into strips about 6 inches long and from ½ to 2 inches wide, depending on your preference. If you like, pinch the center of each strip to create a bow-like shape.

Deep fry in hot oil that has reached 350° F. It should only take a minute or two for them to turn golden brown. Remove and drain on paper towels.

Sprinkle with confectioners sugar before serving.

NEW YORK-STYLE CHEESECAKE

This is the classic New York-style cheesecake and although it's not a true Bartolini recipe, both Mom and Zia liked the cheesecake enough to make it for themselves, so, it kinda qualifies. It is a bit more involved to prepare than most cheesecakes but, I promise, it is well worth the effort. You and your guests will love it.

Over the years, I've served it with sliced kiwi fruit, fresh berries, and a raspberry sauce (p. 196) which, today, would be called a coulis. Try it and you can decide what to call it.

INGREDIENTS

16 oz cream cheese, softened
1 lb cottage cheese, creamed
1½ cup sugar
4 eggs, slightly beaten
3 TBS cornstarch

3 TBS flour
1½ TBS lemon juice
1 tsp lemon zest
1 tsp pure vanilla extract
½ cup butter, melted
16 oz sour cream

DIRECTIONS

Pre-heat oven to 325° F. Thoroughly grease a 9 inch spring form pan.

Using a stand mixer, beat together the cream cheese and cottage cheese at high speed until well combined and smooth.

Gradually add the sugar and then the eggs.

Reduce the speed to low before adding the corn starch, flour, lemon juice, lemon zest, and vanilla.

When well-mixed, add the melted butter and sour cream and beat on low until combined.

Pour the batter into the greased pan and place on the center rack of the preheated oven. Bake for 70 minutes or until cake is firm around the edges.

Turn off the oven and let the cake stand in the oven for 2 hours.

Remove from the oven and allow to cool on a counter for at least 2 hours more.

Refrigerate at least 3 hours before serving.

Garnish with fresh berries or the sauce of your choice.

RASPBERRY SAUCE

The raspberry sauce is my own creation, though the framboise is a recent addition. With or without the liqueur, it is one tasty sauce. Use it with this cheesecake, on ice cream, or just about anything else you like.

INGREDIENTS

12 oz fresh raspberries
3 oz sugar
2 TBS water
splash of Framboise (optional)
pinch of salt

DIRECTIONS

Place the ingredients in a small sauce pan over med-low heat.

Cook until the sugar is melted and the berries have dissolved somewhat.

Place mixture into a food processor or blender and process until smooth.

Strain mixture through a fine sieve.

Discard solids and refrigerate the covered sauce before use.

Should last in the fridge for 3 or 4 days, 30 days if frozen.

Paul, Ron,
Bill, & Me

MOM'S CROSTATA

We could always count on Mom to prepare several treats for the Christmas holiday. Though she started making chocolate candies in her retirement, she always made sure that there were plenty of biscotti and a crostata for Christmas Day. For me, it wouldn't have been Christmas without either being present, no matter what else she had prepared — the platter of ravioli notwithstanding.

Mom often used 2 different jams when making her *crostate*. It's your choice whether to use 1 or 2 jams as a topping. The pastry dough is a common shortbread recipe but any shortbread pastry recipe will do.

INGREDIENTS

FOR THE PASTRY

½ cup confectioners sugar
1 cup unsalted butter, room temperature
¼ tsp salt

2 cups all-purpose flour
an egg yolk and water wash

FOR THE FILLING

Jam/preserves, amount depending upon the crostata's size and whether 2 flavors are to be used. The jam should be from ¼ to ⅓ inch deep, more if you like.

DIRECTIONS

Pre-heat oven to 350° F.

Using a food processor or stand mixer, combine the sugar, butter, and salt.

Slowly add the flour and continue to mix until a dough forms.

Turn on to a lightly floured board and begin kneading, adding more flour if needed.

Reserve a small portion of dough to be used for the lattice.

Roll the dough between 2 sheets of wax paper until about ⅛ inch thick and slightly larger than the tart pan or baking sheet.

Carefully remove one sheet of wax paper and place the dough on to the tart pan, paper-side up. Gently press the dough to fit the contours of the pan. Remove the remaining sheet of wax paper. Trim the excess dough and add to the reserve.

Use an offset spatula to spread the jam, evenly covering the pastry dough. Roll out the reserved pastry dough as you did for the crust. Cut the dough into strips.

Starting at one end, diagonally place the strips across the tart.

Once completed, work from the other side placing strips diagonally in the opposite direction, creating a lattice in the process.

Use the egg wash to lightly coat the lattice and any of the exposed crust.

Bake in the lower third of a pre-heated oven for 30 minutes or until crust and lattice are lightly browned.

Allow to cool before cutting. Serve at room temperature.

ZIA MARIOLA'S APPLE CAKE

This cake is a good one, moist and not too sweet. It's well-traveled, too. It's my Zia Mariola's recipe and was given to my cousin Donna. She, in turn, gave it to her mother-in-law, my Zia Lea, who then gave it to me. Now I'm passing it along to you and, believe me, you'll be glad I did.

Zia Mariola served the cake with a sprinkling of confectioners sugar instead of frosting. I serve it with a drizzle of salted caramel sauce. The salted caramel recipe is next.

INGREDIENTS

1¾ cups sugar
¾ cup oil
3 eggs
½ tsp salt
2 cup all-purpose flour
1 tsp baking soda
1 tsp cinnamon
1 tsp vanilla

4 or 5 apples, peeled, cored, sliced thin
1 cup raisins (pre-soak in warm water
        for 30 minutes)
1 cup chopped walnuts, divided
confectioners sugar - optional
salted caramel sauce for serving
        optional - recipe p 201

DIRECTIONS

Pre-heat oven to 350° F.

Place all ingredients -- except apples, raisins, and nuts -- in a large mixing bowl and beat with a spoon until well-blended. Batter will be stiff.

Add the apples, raisins, and half of the nuts to the bowl and stir until evenly distributed.

Pour into a well-greased 9 X 13" baking dish. Sprinkle the top with the remaining nuts.

Bake in a pre-heated 350° F oven for 45 minutes. It's done when a toothpick inserted into the center is clean when removed.

Allow to cool before dusting with confectioners/powdered sugar and serving.

SALTED CARAMEL SAUCE

The apple cake is delicious when served just as my Zia does, with a sprinkle of powdered sugar and nothing more. On the other hand, there's something about the combination of apples with caramel. This salted caramel sauce pairs perfectly with her cake. Gilding the lily? You betcha!

INGREDIENTS

1 cup sugar
6 TBS butter, cubed
½ cup heavy cream, room
        temperature
2 tsp kosher salt

DIRECTIONS

Pour sugar into a medium sauce pan over med-high heat.

Stir the sugar as it begins to melt and continue to do so until it begins to boil. Stop stirring the moment it begins to boil.

Watch for the sugar to change to an amber color. If need be, swirl the liquid in the pan but no stirring.

Once the sugar turns amber in color, reduce heat to medium, add the butter and whisk vigorously until melted and fully blended.

Remove from heat, gradually add the cream, whisking all the while. Once blended, add the salt and continue to whisk until fully mixed.

Set aside to cool for a few minutes before pouring into a sealable container for storage in the fridge where it will keep for a couple of weeks.

Gently warm before serving.

ZUPPA INGLESE

It would not have been Christmas without Mom's Zuppa Inglese being served after the holiday dinner. She made 2 versions. One for the adults, in which a pastry brush was used to paint the lady fingers with a mixture of whiskey, sweet vermouth, and grenadine. The lady fingers in the version for us kids were painted with grenadine alone. Either way, there were no complaints at the table.

The original recipe used 36 egg yolks, though I've pared this one down to 12. One thing about making this custard is that the eggs must be stirred constantly. Fail to do so and you'll end up with a lumpy mess. A custard of 12 eggs should take about 20 minutes to form. For 36 egg yolks, you'll need to keep stirring for about 45 minutes, and that is a problem, but the women of the two-flat rose to the occasion. Working in our kitchen Mom, Nonna, and Zia moved the kitchen table over to the side of the stove. Once the yolks were placed in the huge enamel pot, one sat at the table's edge and started stirring. The other 2 women played cards, *briscola*, at the opposite end of the table. All 3 enjoyed a glass of wine as they talked and laughed throughout the process. After 10 minutes or so, the 3 rotated and another took her place at the stove. In the end, there was enough Zuppa Inglese for everyone, young and old, seated at the table for Christmas Dinner -- and the ladies had a good time preparing it.

Notes:
There's no need to buy a double boiler if you haven't one. Place a couple of inches of water in a saucepan over low to med-low heat. Put the ingredients in a bowl large enough to lay on top of the saucepan without falling in. The boiling water should never touch the bottom of the bowl.

Following this recipe, you will create a Zuppa Inglese exactly like Mom did every Christmas. You can also make a rather impressive looking trifle, if you like. Using a trifle dish, stand lady fingers on-end to form the outer wall and, for the interior, begin with a little custard on the bottom before alternating layers of lady fingers and custard. Liquor may be added to the internal lady fingers, if you like. Top off the trifle with a layer of freshly whipped cream and refrigerate until ready to serve.

INGREDIENTS

12 egg yolks
zest of 1 lemon
¾ cup sugar
1 cup heavy whipping cream
1 cup half-and-half
lady fingers (thinly sliced pound
       cake may be substituted)

LIQUOR

whiskey
sweet Vermouth
grenadine Syrup

DIRECTIONS

Place all ingredients, except the lady fingers and liquors in the top-half of a double boiler or in a mixing bowl as indicated previously. Use a whisk to thoroughly combine.

Place a couple of inches of water in the bottom-half of the boiler, reassemble the double boiler, and heat over a low to med-low heat. Do not allow the water to touch the inner pot's bottom.

Stir constantly, making sure to scrape the bowl's sides & bottom in the process.

After 20 to 25 minutes, the custard should be thick enough to coat the back of a spoon.

Remove from heat and pour the custard through a sieve to remove any bits of zest.

Combine a few ounces of the liquors and set aside. For a more spirited dessert, use more whiskey.

Ladle enough custard to coat the bottom of a serving dish. Place a layer of lady fingers into the dish and dress with as much liquor as you prefer.

Repeat the process at least twice. Make sure to reserve enough custard to apply a final coating of custard to "top off" the dish.

Refrigerate, covered, for several hours or overnight.

MISCELLANY

Marina,   Mom,   Giuseppe,   Dad,   Darlene,   Donna, Paul, Sr, Justin
       Zia Lea   Paul, Jr,   Rhonda,   Dionne,   Michael

CHICAGO-STYLE GIARDINIERA

In mid-summer, with the farmers markets fully stocked and bustling, the time is right for preserving fruits and vegetables. Pickling is a great way to do it. In Italy pickling is often called *sotto aceto. A* wide variety of vegetables are preserved in this way. Sometimes, a mix of vegetables are prepared, along with some peppers, and the result is called *giardiniera.* Served as a salad or accompaniment, you can usually find it among the antipasti or insalati. In the States, the recipes are pretty much the same, though local chilies have been substituted for those used overseas. Here, in Chicago, we've added a bit more heat and dropped a couple ingredients, resulting in a giardiniera that is more condiment than antipasto. It has become a staple of most sandwich shops and, in some circles, it's almost a sacrilege to order an Italian beef sandwich without a healthy scoop of giardiniera to top it off, but that's not all. Good giardiniera makes a great topping for any sandwich, as well as for burgers, hot dogs, and brats while a healthy sprinkling of it can elevate even the most lackluster of pizzas.

This is a great recipe and has been well-received by friends and family alike. One word of caution, however, because this giardiniera contains oil, it must not be canned. Don't worry. I've yet to have someone tell me that an open container of this giardiniera "went bad." It tends to disappear rather quickly.

INGREDIENTS

8 jalapeños, chopped (for more heat,
    serranos may be substituted)
½ large cauliflower, cut into florets
2 carrots, diced
2 celery stalks, diced
1 green bell pepper, diced
1 red bell pepper, diced
2 sweet banana peppers, diced
1 sweet onion, diced

½ cup kosher salt
3 cloves garlic, minced
2½ tsp dried oregano
1 tsp red pepper flakes
½ tsp celery seeds
black pepper, to taste
½ cup cider vinegar
½ cup white vinegar
½ cup extra virgin olive oil
½ cup vegetable/canola oil

DIRECTIONS

Combine vegetables and salt in a large container Add enough water to cover, stir, cover, and refrigerate for at least 12 hours.

Strain vegetables from brine, rinse well, and set aside.

In a large glass bowl, add garlic and remaining seasonings.

To that bowl, add the vinegars and stir until well-mixed. Whisk the solution while adding the oils.

Add the reserved, brined vegetables into the bowl and gently mix until well-coated.

At this point, the giardiniera may be left, covered, in the bowl or transferred to clean jars. Either way, it must be refrigerated for 48 hours before serving.

Due to its oil content, this giardiniera must not be canned. Store it in the refrigerator, instead, where it will keep for several weeks.

MOM'S TOMATO ANTIPASTI

In mid-summer Grandpa's garden started to come into its own, his tomatoes leading the way. Hardly a day went by without some tomato dish gracing our dinner tables. Memories of those tomato dishes are why I grow tomatoes every summer. These antipasti top the list.

INGREDIENTS

2 or 3 large ripe tomatoes, evenly
 sliced
1 small can of anchovies in oil, drained
 and separated into fillets
2 TBS chopped fresh basil

2 TBS chopped fresh parsley
extra virgin olive oil
red wine vinegar
salt & pepper, to taste
Pecorino Romano or Parmigiano
 Reggiano, grated - optional

DIRECTIONS

Arrange the tomato slices in one layer across a serving platter.

Season with salt & pepper.

Separate the platter into halves. Place 1 anchovy on each tomato slice on one of the halves.

Sprinkle the entire platter with the chopped basil and parsley.

Drizzle the entire platter lightly with extra virgin olive oil before adding a splash of red wine vinegar.

Give a light sprinkling of parmesan cheese to the side of the platter that does NOT contain anchovies.

Serve.

PIEDA

Located in the north of Italy, Emilia-Romagna is a collection of provinces, the southern border of which is shared with San Marino and Marche. Dad emigrated from the Republic of San Marino, Mom's family from Marche. Pieda originated in Romagna where it's called *piedina*, but it came to our dinner table via San Marino. It is a simple flatbread, similar to pita or tortillas, and when folded in half, can be filled with lunch meat, cheese, or a variety of greens. My family's favorite was Swiss chard that had been blanched before being sautéed with a little sliced onion in garlic-flavored extra virgin olive oil . No matter how you choose to fill them, pieda are best when served immediately after cooking.

INGREDIENTS

3 cup all-purpose flour
⅓ cup Crisco (vegetable shortening)
1 tsp baking powder
1 cup milk

DIRECTIONS

Place all ingredients in food processor and mix until a ball of dough forms.

Cover with plastic wrap and refrigerate for 30 minutes.

Remove a small amount of dough and, using a rolling-pin, roll it out until it is about 6 inches in diameter and no less than ⅛ inch thick. Repeat, setting rolled discs aside, separated by wax paper.

Cook in a hot, non-stick frying pan over med-high heat. It should only take a few minutes per side. Use a fork to prick any bubbles that may form during cooking. A side is done when it is mottled with brown spots of varying sizes.

Place cooked pieda on a warmed dish in a warm oven until all are finished.

Serve immediately.

SPIANATA

When I was a boy, Mom occasionally treated us all to homemade pizza. She'd make standard pepperoni or sausage pizzas for us kids but Dad's was a special order. His pizza was called spianata and, unlike our kiddie versions, his was topped with only garlic, onion, rosemary, salt and pepper, resembling a rather plain focaccia. Yet, for so few ingredients, it made a very tasty pizza back then, while Zia and I use it today as a perfect accompaniment for any number of dishes.

This starts with what is called a "sponge." Fairly common to many Italian/European breads, a sponge is a mixture of water, yeast, and flour that's allowed to rise overnight. The mixture, in a sense, ferments and the resultant bread is more flavorful, almost sourdough-like. Of course, you needn't start with a sponge but the spianata is so much more flavorful if you do. Once the sponge has "spent the night," the rest of the recipe is pretty straight-forward and you should have no trouble following it.

INGREDIENTS

FOR THE SPONGE
1 cup all-purpose flour
1 cup warm water
1 tsp active yeast

FOR THE SPIANATA
¾ cup olive oil, divided
1 tsp salt
2 cups all-purpose flour

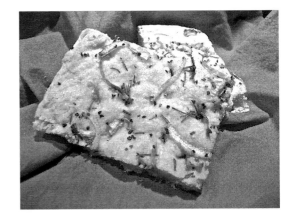

FOR THE TOPPING
½ of a small onion, sliced thin
1 clove garlic, sliced thin or grated
olive oil
3 TBS fresh rosemary, coarsely
*   chopped*
coarse salt & pepper

DIRECTIONS

Proof the yeast in warm water. Add to the flour to make the sponge. Mix well, cover, and set aside. The sponge should be allowed to rise for at least 8 hours but no more than 20. (In my experience, 12 to 16 hours is usually best.) When you are ready to proceed, the sponge's surface should be mottled with bubbles and it should have a strong yeast scent.

To the sponge, add the flour, ½ cup olive oil, and salt. Knead dough for 5 minutes. Dough should not be sticky. If it is, sprinkle with flour and continue kneading until absorbed.

Place dough in an oiled bowl, cover, and let rise until doubled — from 1 to 2 hours.

Punch the dough down, turn it onto a floured work surface, cover with a towel, and let rest for 15 minutes. Meanwhile, coat a 9 x 12" sheet pan with the remaining ¼ cup of olive oil.

After resting 15 minutes, place dough onto the pan and use your fingers to begin stretching it to fit the pan. When it covers about ⅔ of the pan, flip the dough over and continue stretching the dough until the entire pan is covered and there's enough dough to create a ridge around the pan's edge.

Cover with a towel and let rise until doubled again, about 1 hour.

Pre-heat oven to 425° F. Place garlic and onion into a small bowl and moisten lightly with olive oil.

Once doubled, remove towel and, with your fingers, poke the surface of the dough repeatedly. Sprinkle surface with the garlic-onion mixture, rosemary, coarse salt & pepper.

Bake on oven's center rack for about 25 minutes. The spianata should be lightly browned.

Allow to cool slightly before cutting and serving.

JERKY TREATS FOR DOGS

Dogs have played a big role in our lives, no matter where we have lived. While at the two-flat, there were always at least 2 dogs in residence. When we each moved away, it wasn't long before dogs were introduced to our new homes. Photos of some of these dogs have been shared throughout this book.

Skipper, my first dog, was a Christmas gift when I was one month shy of being seven-years-old. At the time, Sis and I were both losing our baby teeth. I was 11 months older and winning this race which, of course, meant more visits by the Tooth Fairy. That spring, Skipper joined the race and began dropping his baby teeth, too. Sis found one and saw it as an opportunity to get another, totally unexpected, visit from the Tooth Fairy That night, she placed the tooth under her pillow, just as she would have done with one of her own. The next morning she awoke and eagerly lifted her pillow, expecting to find her reward from the Tooth Fairy. Instead she found a dog biscuit. One must never try to fool the Tooth Fairy.

I started making jerky treats for Max after reading that a few store-bought jerky treats had caused some dogs to grow gravely ill. They're easy enough to prepare at home and you do not need a dehydrator to make them. Best of all, your dog will love them!

Beef   *Chicken*

Take raw beef, chicken, or salmon and cut into strips of equal length and width. This will ensure that all are dried evenly. If using racks, spray them with cooking spray before individually placing the strips upon them. Place the racks on top of baking sheets to catch the drippings. Without racks, cover the baking sheets with parchment paper or a light coating of cooking spray before placing the strips. Make sure that the strips do not touch each other, no matter what method used. Place the baking sheet(s) in a pre-heated 170° F oven and bake for 6½ hours. Turn over each strip every 2 hours while rotating the trays. When finished, remove, cool, and store in an airtight container in the fridge if to be used in the next few days. Place in the freezer for longer storage.

ONE MORE
FOR THE ROAD

Ron, Grandpa, and Paul
Mom and Bill (foreground)

MANHATTAN COCKTAILS

No collection of Bartolini recipes would be complete without at least mentioning Manhattan cocktails. I don't know why I drink Manhattans back home for I rarely, if ever, drink them anywhere else. Nevertheless, for decades, Manhattans are the house cocktail when I visit -- and I don't drink alone. Ron, the Max Whisperer, is sure to join me when he isn't roaming the countryside with his faithful companion. He wasn't around, however, one afternoon about 25 years ago. I'd gone down to the beach to get some sun. Like much of Michigan, huge bluffs face the lake and the path to the beach is down a very steep hill. I was there about 30 minutes when Zia appeared carrying a pitcher of Manhattans and 2 glasses. After about 15 minutes, as we sat sipping our cocktails, Mom appeared carrying another pitcher of Manhattans and 2 glasses. After a good laugh, the 3 of us spent the afternoon together, sitting on the beach, sipping Manhattans. Thank heavens this took place before the Video Age and smartphones for there is no footage of the 3 of us struggling to get up that hill, empty pitchers in hand, laughing the entire way.

INGREDIENTS

1 oz whiskey
1½ oz sweet vermouth
ice
lemon twist or Maraschino cherry

DIRECTIONS

Pour whiskey and sweet vermouth into a cocktail shaker and shake to combine.

Use a lemon twist to rub the edge of a rocks glass. Fill with ice.

Pour cocktail over ice in the rocks glass.

Squeeze a lemon twist into the glass before dropping it into the cocktail.

Serve.

*** Mom preferred her Manhattan served with a Maraschino cherry instead of the lemon twist.

Note: Unlike our cocktail, a true Manhattan is served 2:1, that's 2 parts whiskey to 1 part sweet vermouth, along with a shake or 2 of (Agostino) bitters. A lemon twist or cherry is then added.

WORTH A THOUSAND WORDS

Dad at the USO (c WWII)

Grandma Erselia's Parents and Two Sisters (c 1926)

Grandma Erselia's Sister and Brother-in-Law (c 1928)

Grandma Erselia's Sister

Grandpa Bart's Brother and Bride, in Paris (c 1928)

Grandpa Bart's Uncle Ben and Family

Grandpa Bart's Uncle Victor

INDICES

Mom, Me, and Zia Lea

STORIES

RECIPES

RECIPES

RECIPES

RECIPES

RECIPES

RECIPES

RECIPES

Grandpa Bart

RECIPES

FROM THE BARTOLINI

KITCHENS

Made in the USA
San Bernardino, CA
15 November 2015